To my husband, Peter Todd

The Joice Alley steps as seen from Pine Street

Lunchtime Walks in Downtown San Francisco

Gail Todd

WILDERNESS PRESS
BERKELEY

Photos by the author except as noted
Maps by Meridian Mapping
Design by Margaret Copeland
Cover design by Jaan Hitt
Front cover photos ©1998 by John Elk III
Back cover photos ©1998 by Alisha Todd

Library of Congress Card Number 98-24699
ISBN 0-89997-217-9

Manufactured in the United States of America
Published by   Wilderness Press
                 2440 Bancroft Way
                 Berkeley, CA 94704
                 (800) 443-7227
                 FAX (510) 548-1355
                 mail@wildernesspress.com
                 Visit our website www.wildernesspress.com

                 Contact us for a free catalog

Front cover photos (clockwise from top): Chinatown window display; Telegraph
        Hill and Coit Tower; San Francisco Museum of Modern Art
Back cover photo (bottom): View of Transamerica Pyramid from pier
        along Embarcadero

♻ Printed on recycled paper, 20% post-consumer waste

Library of Congress Cataloging-in-Publication Data
Todd, Gail.
Lunchtime walks in downtown San Francisco / by Gail Todd.--1st ed.
                p.   cm.
        Includes bibliographical references and index.
        ISBN 0-89997-217-9 (alk. paper)
        1. Walking--California--San Francisco--Guidebooks. 2. Hiking-
-California--San Francisco--Guidebooks. 3. San Francisco (Calif)-
-Guidebooks I. Title.
GV199.42.C22S278   1998
917.94'610453--dc21
                                                        98-24699
                                                           CIP

Table of Contents

Acknowledgments

First and foremost my gratitude goes to my husband, Peter Todd, whose knowledge of the most wonderful places to walk, excitement about getting there, and insistence upon returning again and again to observe the most minute details have added immeasurably both to this book and to the fun of writing it.

Thanks to my friend Judith Tannenbaum with whom I have shared so many writing adventures. Her dedication to quality is a ever-renewing source of inspiration. I am grateful to her for her careful reading of the manuscript.

Thanks to Caroline and Tom Winnett for giving me the opportunity to publish this book, and additionally to Tom for applying his well-honed editing skills to my work.

Thanks to Barbara Jackson of Meridian Mapping for turning my hand-drawn sketches into real maps, and to the staff of Wilderness Press for skillfully and professionally accomplishing the many tasks involved in the production of this book.

Thanks to Brooks Camera for taking time and care with my photos. I'm sorry I bounced a check in 1966. I won't do it again.

Thanks to my dear friend Sylvia Rabiner for her precious friendship this past half century.

Thanks to my dad, Fred Geyzer, for great survival skills.

Thanks to my daughters, Kim and Tamar Todd, for their warm and constant love.

Introduction

I started working for the Bank of America in San Francisco in October 1990 when I was 51 years old. This was my first office job in 29 years. The last time I'd worked in an office, I was a 22 year-old kid working my way through college in New York City.

I've never been good at "day jobs." Instead, I've steered a somewhat peripatetic path through life. During my 29 non-office years, I wrote computer books for Osborne/McGraw-Hill, ran my own technical writing business, taught school, published poetry, bummed around Europe, got married, and had two kids. (Events not listed in order.)

In the fall of 1990, my younger daughter was busily filling out her college applications, and I realized I would soon have two kids in Eastern colleges. (I started thinking of "Eastern college" as one word "easterncollege.") I added up all the figures for tuitions, room, and board, and saw I was adding up big bucks. I decided my rambling days had come to an end. It was time to get a regular job, so I would know exactly how much money was coming in.

I've had my job in downtown San Francisco at the Bank of America's world headquarters for seven years now. At first, it was really hard for me to sit still for so long each day. About two o'clock in the afternoon, I would start to twitch. At three I would think "I'm outta here," and stroll around the block, pretending my dog Puppy was with me snuffling up sidewalk scraps.

For a while, I tried to get exercise at lunch by going to the gym. But my third week at the gym, I tripped on the treadmill while strapping a walkman on my arm and scraped all the skin off the front of both legs—thighs to ankles. (The treadmill kept going; I didn't). Then, the next week, I wrenched my knee; then my shoulder. Finally, I found myself in the office of the Berkeley Orthopaedic Medical Group listening to the doctor's somber advice.

"Ms. Todd," he said, "*please*, never go to the gym again."

I didn't. Instead, I started walking at lunch almost every day. At first I walked to places I knew, but then I just started "setting out" feeling the thrill of the explorer venturing into uncharted territory. Little by little, I started to realize how beautiful, exciting, and spirit-renewing downtown San Francisco can be.

The lunchtime walks calmed me down and refreshed me for the afternoon. Occasionally, I could even sit through meetings without fidgeting.

My walks varied in length because some days I could only spare a few minutes, while other days, I could stretch the standard lunch "hour" and venture further. I wandered around City Lights Books, trudged up and down the Filbert and Greenwich steps, broke a sweat climbing Nob Hill to view Grace Cathedral, barked at the sea lions at Pier 39, explored Chinatown, and chomped down sweets from the Victoria Pastry Company in North Beach.

Then, in 1992, something exciting happened. In 1989, a year before I started working at the bank, the Loma Prieta quake had delivered a fatal blow to the Embarcadero Freeway, and in 1992, it was torn down. After the quake-damaged freeway was razed, the once-dreary San Francisco

As the freeway crumbled, the skyline emerged

waterfront was reborn as a sun-filled walker's paradise. Not only that, but city views previously truncated by concrete structures now opened into the Bay and far beyond.

The Embarcadero Freeway had originally been slated to circle the waterfront from the Bay Bridge to the Golden Gate, but in 1959 citizen protest stopped construction of the freeway after it marched across Market to Broadway. For years, the traffic-choked structure had shadowed the shoreline between the Bay Bridge and North Beach. In the three years between the quake and the demolition, cars were replaced by midnight skaters, who climbed the now-silent structure to twirl along its ghostly flanks. Then, in 1992, the waterfront was liberated.

Mostly, I walked alone, but sometimes a Ukrainian émigré named Jenny went with me. One day, Jenny said to me, as we ambled down the Filbert steps together, "You should write these walks down and put them in a book." I decided to do it.

This book is about my lunchtime walks.

THE WALKS

All the walks start from one of three downtown landmarks:

- The Ferry Building, past Market at the Embarcadero

- The Bank of America world headquarters building at Kearny and California

- The cable car turnaround at Powell and Market.

Since I work at the Bank of America world headquarters building, many walks start from there. Specifically, they start from the "Banker's Heart," a blobby black sculpture on the Bank of America plaza at the corner of Kearny and California. The sculpture was created by Masayuki Nagare, and its real name is *Transcendence*. You can decide for yourself which name suits it better. The sculpture has recently been placed atop a little lawn to discourage the over-eager skateboarders who occasionally used to attack its gleaming flanks.

Within each starting location, walks are listed roughly from short to long.

Feel free to experiment and tailor the walks to your own job location. You can start a walk in one place and end it someplace else. What's a "miniwalk" from one starting place can become a "marathon" from another. Walking is *not* an exact science and exploring is part of the fun. You're not going to get lost in downtown San Francisco. And you're not going to get hypothermia either—although you may dispute this if the fog rolls in.

All the walks are to places that are either free to visit or at least have a free day once a month. But that doesn't mean you can't spend a bundle before you get back to work. For example, if you walk to a great bookstore or gallery, you can end up spending a week's salary—or more.

Some of the walks take only a few minutes. Others can take a couple of hours. Times are approximate—you will encounter red lights and crowded streets. All time estimates are "round trip" for me, including the time I spent waiting for red lights. Don't jaywalk. Don't get run over.

The applicable question here is "How fast do I walk?" I think the oxymoron "brisk stroll" tells it all. Generally, I walk at a pretty good clip. Or at least I think I do. My grandfather once told me that he realized he was getting old when he would be out taking a brisk walk and would see people slowly strolling past him. This hasn't happened to me more than once or twice.

Time estimates are for the walking part only and do not include the time I spend to stop and explore. The reason is that there's no way for *me* to

The Banker's Heart before *skateboard-proofing*

The Banker's Heart after *skateboard-proofing*

estimate how long you will spend looking around a church, shop, museum, or gallery. If you get lost in a great bookstore, you can easily spend the whole afternoon.

Some walks—such as walks to art galleries or concerts—have a goal. You get some exercise, see or hear something special, and walk back. For others—for example, a walk through Chinatown— the walk itself is the whole event.

I take you through the same streets in several walks, but that's one of the great pleasures of walking, going over the same ground until it's familiar. The reason the book is organized this way is that these are *lunchtime* walks, so I didn't want to say "Let's do Civic Center. Allow four hours." Instead I broke the walks down into chunks that you *can* cover in one lunchtime. Then you can come back another day to do another chunk.

And what about the weather? San Francisco is known as a mighty foggy city. But in my walks, it always seems sunny. The reason is that the morning fog has usually burned off by noon and the afternoon fog hasn't rolled in yet. Usually, that is.

Although I tried to be thorough, San Francisco is a changing city, and I'm sure I've left out some good places. So, I welcome letters—politely worded versions of "Hey, dummy, you left out the best walk. Let me tell you about...".

Have fun and don't worry too much about getting back to work on time.

MAP LEGEND

Start   Start of walk

=====   Route

—————   Other streets

▬ - ▬ - ▬   Cable Car Line

▬ ▬ ▬   Route over cable car line

|||||||||||||||| Stairway

- - - - - - - -   Path

▭   Walkway, walkover

▬▬▬   Freeway

→   Walking direction

⊏   Turnaround

● ▭   Point of interest

✿   Fountains, Monuments, Sculptures, Statues

▦   Parks, Playgrounds, Plazas, Squares

] [Bridge

‿   Tunnel opening

The arrows used to indicate the walking direction sometimes indicate a sharp turn, a bend or a slight jog, indicating a change in direction.

These arrows indicate walking to and fro, along the same route.

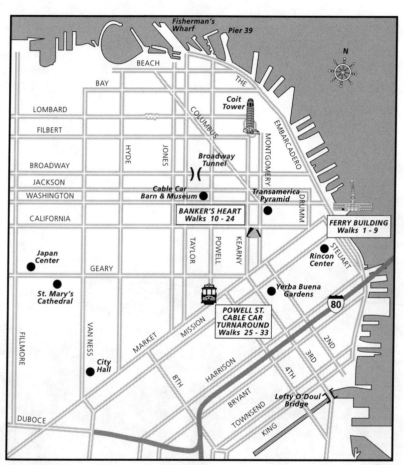

Locator Map

Looking back at the city from Pier 7

The Ferry Building, past Market on the Embarcadero

WALK 1   Ferry Plaza & Environs

It's hard to imagine now, but at one time the 235-foot-high clock tower of the Ferry Building was considered the very symbol of San Francisco in much the same way that the Golden Gate Bridge is today. Before the Golden Gate and Bay bridges spanned the Bay, you probably took the ferry to come to San Francisco. In fact, over 100,000 commuters a day did just that. In the 1920s, people made 50 million ferry trips a year to and from San Francisco.

Designed by architect Arthur Page Brown and modeled after the Cathedral Tower of Seville in Spain, the Ferry Building opened on July 13, 1898. It survived the great quake and fire of 1906, it survived the Loma Prieta quake of 1989, and it is surviving today, given new strength and life by the demolition of the Embarcadero Freeway, which reunited the city with its waterfront roots.

The Ferry Building is surrounded by plazas—Ferry Plaza, Justin Herman Plaza, Embarcadero Plaza, and it's not easy to tell exactly where one plaza ends and the next one begins, but who cares.

The Ferry Building tower

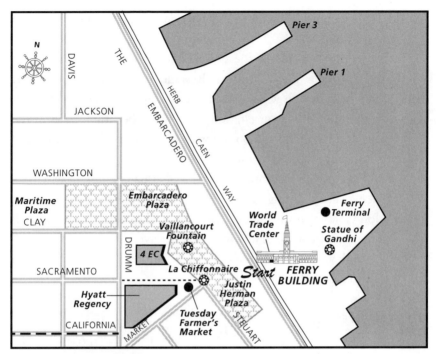

Ferry Plaza and Environs

Plan to take this walk on a Tuesday, so you can see the Farmers' Market at the foot of Market Street, which operates from 11 A.M. to 3 P.M. except in the winter. (A larger, weekend Farmers' Market recently moved from directly in front of the Ferry Building to the Embarcadero at Green Street.)

WALKING TIME

No set time. Plan to spend about an hour strolling around. The point of this walk is to be out in the air, to see the boats, the bridge, the fishermen, the people of the city.

FERRY PLAZA

There is nothing much to see inside the Ferry Building, or inside the adjacent World Trade Center, so plan to spend all your time outdoors. (The exception is the International Children's Art Museum inside the

World Trade Center. It's open Monday through Friday from 9 A.M. to 5 P.M., and it's free.)

To get to the Bay side of the Ferry Building walk around it to the south, and starting at Pier 2 (Sinbad's Restaurant) slowly wend your way back along the Bay. You will see fishermen fishing leisurely off the railings, other strollers like yourself, and staggeringly beautiful views of the Bay Bridge and its anchorage on Yerba Buena Island. It's a mighty nice place to stop and just do nothing.

You will also see an inspiring statue of Mahatma Gandhi, in which he looks as if he were planning to stroll right across the Bay. The inscription reads "Non violence is the greatest force at the disposal of mankind. It is the supreme law. By it alone can mankind be saved."

As you walk around by Gabbiano's Restaurant, you will see the actual Ferry Terminal complete with ferries.

JUSTIN HERMAN PLAZA

When you have had your fill of the Bay in all its glory, return to the front of the Ferry Building and cross the Embarcadero. (At this writing, I had to take a makeshift "detour" to cut through the Ferry Building, but

The much-criticized Vaillancourt Fountain

the structure is slated for renovation, and plans are in place for a central atrium that opens out onto the Bay.)

In front of you and stretching to your right is Justin Herman Plaza with its infamous *Vaillancourt Fountain*. When this precast concrete structure was unveiled in 1971, people commented that it looked like the freeway had tumbled down. Now that the freeway *has* been torn down, leaving the Plaza drenched in magnificent sunshine, the fountain seems to commemorate that event.

Justin Herman Plaza has lots of wonderful places to sit—if you don't insist on actual benches. There are many impromptu concerts here, and, on Friday evenings, wild inline skaters do things that would definitely put me in a body cast for the rest of my life.

Check out the *Vaillancourt Fountain*. Aesthetics aside, the great thing about the this structure is that you can actually walk *in* it. In fact, large flat blocks exist for that very purpose. As I walked along under the spray, I kept thinking "This isn't allowed," but actually it is! You can pretty much get as wet as you want.

From November through January, there is also a miniature ice-skating rink here.

Just north of Justin Herman Plaza is Embarcadero Plaza, essentially a large "grassy knoll" to use an infamous expression. It would be a great place to snooze except that the grass often seems wet. My theory is that this is to keep the homeless from sleeping here.

Tourists studying the map on the fancy JCDecaux French toilet

Where Market Street terminates at Justin Herman Plaza you can find one of the city's new JCDecaux French toilets, useful not only for its "facilities," but also for the excellent tourist map on its broad green flanks. In the same area, you will find the gigantic stainless steel and epoxy sculpture *La Chiffonniere* by Jean Dubuffet. If I remember my high-school French correctly, a "chiffonniere" is a rag picker.

For lunch, you can pick up munchies at the Farmers' Market (on Tuesdays). The Tuesday market is definitely "upscale," more known for fancy chips and dips than for cabbages. Or you can get a bite at one of the many take-out eateries that line the west side of the Plaza and the pedestrian extension of Sacramento Street. The main thing is, stay out-doors!

This short walk was shown to me one day after work by my husband Pete, and it's actually my favorite. Different each time, it's one walk in the sun, another in the fog. It is the only walk that gives you that "I'm just a speck of dust in the universe" feeling, an awareness that, paradoxically, always exhilarates rather than diminishes.

Built in 1990, Pier 7 is a public access pier, designed to give San Franciscans a place to fish, enjoy the view, and, apparently, snooze. Extending past the surrounding structures, it provides a stunning 360-degree panorama of the city and the waters that surround it. As you

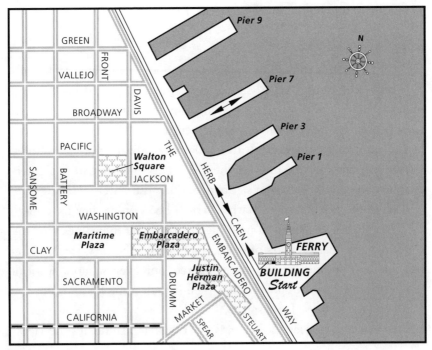

Pier 7

slowly turn and look, you leave the "feel" of downtown totally behind. You can actually forget where you are.

WALKING TIME

About twenty minutes round trip just getting there and back. Allow more time to enjoy your surroundings.

GETTING THERE

From the Ferry Building on the Embarcadero walk north on Herb Caen Way, which will be jammed with skaters, strollers, bikers, and some very peppy skateboarders. You will come to the Pier 1 Deli and, if you wish, you can walk down Pier 1, which has its own pretty views and benches. A number of ferries leave from here.

Between Piers 3 and 5 is the historic Santa Rosa Ferry, built in 1927. Although mostly used for offices, the ferry is open to the public and you can wander around and even go up to the roof deck. I did, and learned that ferries haven't changed much in three quarters of a century.

Continue on Herb Caen Way to Pier 7.

PIER 7

At the entrance to the Pier, make sure to look at the large pink granite bench/sculptures. In fact, sit down on them. Designed by Oakland sculptor Steve Gillman, these bench/sculptures let you look through their centers to the Bay waters rushing beneath.

Continue down the Pier. With its plank boardwalk and its teal blue Victorian lampposts and railings, the Pier seems to emerge from a different time and place. Victorian slat benches line the way.

Unlike the South Beach Marina, which hosts only a few fishermen, Pier 7 is alive with busy and noisy people dropping their lines into the water. I have heard reports of crabs, anchovies, sting rays, sharks, king fish, halibut, sardines, smelt, stripers, perch, and even salmon. A lot of different languages are spoken here. The fish-cleaning fountains at the Pier's end are well-used and smelly.

Pier 7's claim to fame, however, is not the great fishing; it's the view.

Fishermen on Pier 7

Looking toward the Bay, you will see the Bay Bridge to the right. The center anchorage is very visible. This massive concrete block rises 508 feet from bedrock to top, with 281 feet extending above the water. Yerba Buena and Treasure Island seem close. Further left is Angel Island. Behind the islands, you can see Oakland, the Berkeley Hills, and Point Richmond. On a very clear day, you can even see the top of Mt. Diablo rising behind Oakland. Scanning further left, you can view the Richmond-San Rafael Bridge and, finally, very faintly, you can see Red Rock, San Francisco's northernmost point.

Now turn around. The vista sweeps from Telegraph Hill and Coit Tower rising to your right, to the Transamerica Pyramid directly in front of you, to the Ferry Building and the city spreading south of Market. It's impressive.

GETTING BACK

Return the way you came.

Rincon Center &
the Bay Bridge Anchorage

This is two walks—one short and one long. If you're pressed for time, you can just explore Rincon Center—once the Rincon Annex Post Office. If you're not pressed and want a longer walk, continue on to see where the Bay Bridge anchors into Rincon Hill at Bryant and Beale.

When I first came to San Francisco in 1965, the Rincon Annex was where you raced to mail your tax forms a few minutes before midnight on April 15. Today Rincon Annex has metamorphosed into Rincon Center, an "art deco moderne" complex containing restaurants, shops, offices, luxury apartments, and even a post office!

Designed by architect Gilbert S. Underwood in the Moderne style, Rincon Annex opened in 1940. In 1941, Russian-born artist Anton Refregier won a WPA contest to create murals for the new post office and was paid the then princely sum of $26,000 for his 400 square feet of art. Work on the 26 murals stopped during World War II and did not resume until 1946, and the project wasn't completed until 1948. The murals are not actually frescos, but rather "case in tempera" on white gesso over plaster wall.

Refregier did not create a "pretty" art work. Instead, he showed San Francisco history with all its problems, including prejudice against Chinese and mistreatment of Native Americans. One panel, for example, is called "Vigilante Days," another "Beating the Chinese." Refregier stepped on a lot of toes, so 92 changes were made to the murals before they were deemed acceptable. In 1953, during the McCarthy era, a resolution was introduced into the U.S. Congress to destroy the murals entirely because of their Communist tone, but the resolution was defeated and the art works survived.

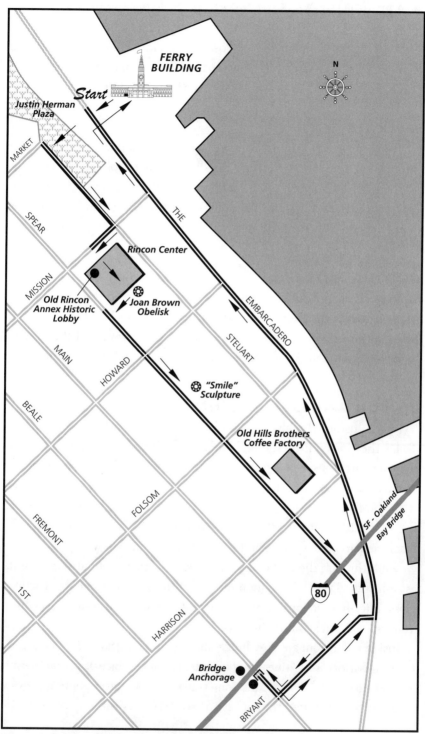

Rincon Center and the Bay Bridge Anchorage

In 1978, the Rincon Annex Post Office closed. The following year Refregier died in Moscow as he was painting a mural on top of a medical clinic. And in 1986 work was begun on Rincon Center.

WALKING TIME

If you are going only to Rincon Center, walking time is barely five minutes each way from the Ferry Building. If you're going on to view the Bay Bridge anchorage, add an additional walking time of 15 minutes each way, for a total walking time of 40 minutes. Add to this the time you plan to spend in Rincon Center.

GETTING THERE

From the Ferry Building, cross the Embarcadero to the south side of Market Street. Turn left at Steuart and walk one block to Mission. Cross Mission, turn right on Mission, and walk to the entrance of the historic lobby—old Rincon Annex preserved as part of new Rincon Center.

RINCON ANNEX AND CENTER

In the historical lobby you can view all of Anton Refregier's murals. Today they look a little stiff and fairly tame, though there are some hammers and sickles sprinkled around. The lobby also displays cases full of artifacts discovered during excavation for the new center. Recovered from the many boarding houses and shops that burned during the great fire of 1906 are items of all sorts—pencils, bits of rope, coal shovels, machine parts, safety pins, and shoe soles, to name a few.

Walk through the lobby into the Rincon Center skylit atrium with its astonishing 85-foot-high fountain/sculpture *Rain Column* by Richard Hass. Fifty-five gallons of water a minute pour down from the ceiling. You will think it's raining indoors.

Inside the atrium are busy lunch shops (from burgers and shake joints, to pizza parlors, to Chinese restaurants, to fancy places), people sitting around eating and talking, and sometimes a piano player pounding away. The last time I visited the San Francisco SPCA was there too, with its cages of cats. Needless to say, the noise level at lunch is high. In fact, it's one infernal racket in there.

To escape, walk through the atrium to the serene outdoor courtyard beyond. Here is some greenery, pretty teal benches and tables, and a few people quietly reading. In the courtyard's center is an unidentified obelisk decorated with leaping porpoises. It's by artist Joan Brown. (To see more of her artwork, take "Walk 5" and "Walk 6.")

THE BAY BRIDGE ANCHORAGE

If you want to continue on to the Bay Bridge anchorage, turn right in the courtyard and exit on Spear Street. Then walk south on Spear through a busy downtown business district. Just past 201 Spear Terrace you will come upon a lifelike sculpture of a man taking your picture with his camera. It's called *Smile* and was executed by artist J. Seward Johnson, Jr.

Past Folsom, you will walk past the back of the red brick Hills Plaza, the site of the old Hills Brothers coffee factory. Continue on Spear Street, past the Bay Bridge Pump Station, until Spear ends at Bryant. Turn right and then right again at Beale. You will see where the Bay Bridge anchors into San Francisco at Rincon Hill.

So what's so great about the Bay Bridge anchorage? Well, although the Bay Bridge has always played second fiddle to its glamorous sister, Ms. Golden Gate, the Bay Bridge is a truly remarkable engineering feat. Its eight-mile span actually consists of two bridges separated by a tunnel at Yerba Buena Island. The Oakland-to-Yerba Buena part is a cantilever bridge; the San Francisco-to-Yerba Buena part is a double-suspension bridge. (On "Walk 2," you can see where the two suspensions meet.)

Construction of the bridge commenced in 1933 with President Franklin Roosevelt setting off a remote-control blast from Washington D.C. Herbert Hoover called the structure "the greatest bridge yet erected by the human race." Costing $77,600,000 at completion in 1936, the bridge was thought to be the most expensive project in history. The pier connecting the two suspension bridges was sunk deeper than any other structure on earth. The consensus at the time was that the Bay Bridge would be the world's largest bridge for a least a thousand years. It is still the world's longest steel high-level bridge.

At the anchorage, you can see where the two gigantic supporting cables (each consisting of 17,464 wires) anchor into 68,000 cubic yards of reinforced concrete.

What's behind the locked doors in the concrete bunker sitting there? It's the Bay Bridge records. And they look really safe.

Rincon Hill, the home of the anchorage, was once the city's most fashionable district. The term *rincon*, means "inside corner," and Rincon

Smile sculpture on Spear Street

Hill nestled on the inside corner of what then was a cove of the Bay. Today, the Hill has pretty much been leveled, and is effectively obscured by the bridge.

During the 1989 Loma Prieta earthquake, a section of the bridge's upper-level roadway collapsed east of Yerba Buena, resulting in the death of a driver. The bridge was closed for a month for repair. It reopened on November 16 with a pedestrian bridge walk that included Tony Bennett in person singing *I Left My Heart in San Francisco*. I was there.

GETTING BACK

To return, walk east on Bryant to the Embarcadero. Cross. Then walk back to the Ferry Building along Herb Caen Way. This will give you a chance to enjoy the waterfront and a nautical breeze or two before you return to work.

Embarcadero Center, the Hyatt Regency, & the Federal Reserve Buildings

The "big city" skyline that you see today as you drive over the Bay Bridge to San Francisco is actually quite new. Most of the giant skyscrapers have been there only since the Seventies, when the downtown area went through a major urban renewal.

Until 1963, the area around today's Embarcadero Center was a humble produce district, which hovered around Washington Street from Front to Drumm. However, the San Francisco Redevelopment Agency had plans for this area more exalted than carrot and turnip sales. It envisioned a three-part mixed-land use "city within a city." The residential part of this plan eventually became the Golden Gateway apartments and condominiums. The public improvements part became Justin Herman Plaza. And, finally, the commercial part became Embarcadero Center with its 140 shops and restaurants.

Embarcadero Center has worked at being a good neighbor. Its public art collection is impressive, as is the amount of open space it offers to shoppers and strollers. Its aerial walkways let you promenade outdoors for five blocks without having to cross a street.

Construction of the Embarcadero Center took 20 years—from 1968 to 1988. And then, just when everything seemed as renovated and revived as it could get, the Loma Prieta quake hit, the Embarcadero Freeway was demolished, and the waterfront area was reborn all over again with new vistas, a romantic promenade, Canary Island palms, and a brand new construction boom.

Today's Embarcadero Center encompasses not only the four original buildings, but the Hyatt Regency and Park Hyatt hotels, the Old Federal Reserve building, and Embarcadero Center West, another office tower directly south of the Old Federal Reserve building.

During the winter months, Embarcadero Center sets up a real ice-skating rink right in Justin Herman Plaza. (There used to be a plastic one inside of the Hyatt Regency.) Skating isn't free, but watching the skaters is.

At Christmas time, the Center becomes an artwork itself, lit up with 17,000 white lights, which dramatically outline its giant spiky towers.

WALKING TIME

About 45 minutes, not counting time spent exploring the Federal Reserve buildings.

The spiral staircase leading from Justin Herman Plaza to Four Embarcadero Center

GETTING THERE

From the Ferry Building, cross the Embarcadero to Justin Herman Plaza. Just west of the Vaillancourt Fountain is Four Embarcadero Center. A flower-lined outdoor spiral staircase winds from level to level. Climb the staircase to the top.

THE EMBARCADERO CENTER & THE OLD FEDERAL RESERVE BUILDING

The Embarcadero Center is on three levels: the street level, the lobby level, and the promenade level. From the lobby and promenade levels, you can thread from one building to the next on the aerial walkways. You can go all the way from Justin Herman Plaza to Sansome without ever having to worry about cars or traffic lights.

Both indoor and outdoor areas are filled with sculpture, and you can stop at one of the information booths and pick up a brochure that takes you on a self-guided sculpture tour.

For walking, the best level is the Promenade, which is entirely in the open air. Head west (it's the only way you *can* go). From here, you can walk above the city streets with downtown to your south and Embarcadero and Maritime Plazas to your north. There are few shops at this level, but lots of restaurants and outdoor seating (and, oddly, lots of dentists.)

The Promenade's "urban gardens" are planted with poppies, impatiens, and geraniums. There are plenty of stone benches big enough to snooze on and lots of little tables and chairs for brown-baggers.

At Three Embarcadero Center, you can look down at *Sky Tree*, a 29-ton, 54-foot black steel sculpture by Louise Nevelson that is set in a reflecting pool. At One Embarcadero Center, you will come to the Embarcadero Center Cinema, a giant five-screen complex, that opened in July 1995. (You can walk through the cinema and exit onto Maritime Plaza if you want to head into parts north.)

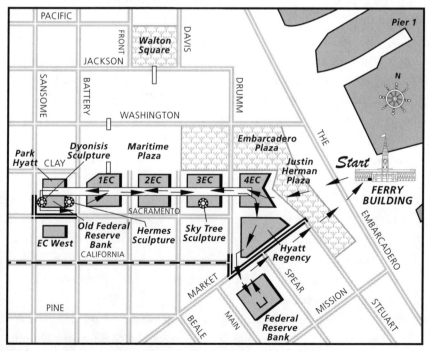

Embarcadero Center, the Hyatt Regency and the Federal Reserve Buildings

Continue west past the theater, and you will soon hear the sound of rushing water. Descend the broad steps—with water flowing on each side—until you exit One Embarcadero Center at street level at the end of Commercial. Walk straight ahead to Sansome. The Old Federal Reserve Bank building will be directly to your left.

Completed in 1924, this impressive building was the original head-quarters of the Twelfth District of the Federal Reserve System. In 1925, during construction of an armored car entrance, workers found the rem-nants of the *Apollo*, a full-rigged sailing schooner, here. Today, artifacts from the ship are on display at the National Maritime Museum in Aquatic Park.

In 1984, the Federal Reserve Bank moved to new digs on Market Street, and the old building, now owned by Embarcadero Center, was totally restored and entered into the National Register of Historic Places. Today, the upper floors are used by a law firm, and the first floor Banking Hall is rented out for events. In fact, you can rent it for a weekend wed-ding for only $4,500.

On a sunny day, the Bank steps are lined with downtowners eating lunch. At the Sansome entrance, you can see the Arman sculpture *Hermes*, an unusual piece of artwork that lets you see through to the inside of the figures. Walk into the Banking Hall, itself. The chandeliers, the 25-foot-high Ionic columns, the walls and floors finished in French and Italian marble, all create the feel of a banking "temple."

Walk around to the Battery Street side to view *Dyonisos*, another Arman sculpture. Then cross Battery and turn left to reenter One Embarcadero Center. This time, go up only to the Lobby Level. Here, as you retrace your steps back toward Justin Herman Plaza, you can peruse the many shops that attract visitors to Embarcadero Center. Alas, these are not fascinating "one of a kind" shops like you'll find at Pier 39, but rather big national stores like The Limited, Liz Claiborne, Casual Corner, and the Footlocker.

Between Three Embarcadero Center and Four Embarcadero Center climb back up to the Promenade Level (you will be passing over Drumm Street). Then turn right to enter the Hyatt Regency Hotel.

THE HYATT REGENCY

The lobby of the Hyatt Regency Hotel is one of my favorite interior spaces. I remember taking my children here—just to look—when they were very little, and they were spellbound.

The huge tiered atrium, the black and gold teardrop elevators sailing up and down, the glassy fountain that you must touch to see if it's really water, the four-ton *Eclipse* sculpture that seems to float weightlessly on the liquid surface, the hundreds of feet of ivy that dangles from ledges above create an overwhelming sense of wonder. (I recently discovered that the dangling ivy is no longer "real," as it once was. Today, it's artificial.)

Atop the Hyatt Regency is the Equinox, San Francisco's only revolving rooftop restaurant. In this very restaurant, about 20 years ago, I was having a drink with my sister-in-law Sandy, enjoying the 360-degree city panorama, when her purse disappeared. We couldn't understand how, since she had been sitting in the interior of a booth the whole time, with her purse against the wall. Finally, we realized that we had rotated away

Outside the Hyatt Regency San Francisco.

Photo by Dennis Anderson

from her purse. (We were moving; the wall wasn't.) We found the purse after a good number of embarrassing searches of other patrons' booths.

To leave the hotel, take the escalator down two flights from the lobby and exit onto Drumm by the big gold revolving doors.

THE NEW FEDERAL RESERVE BANK

What's with these shopping centers and money? The Embarcadero Center is sandwiched between the old and the new Federal Reserve Bank buildings. The San Francisco Shopping Center is around the corner from the former Mint. Maybe there's a message here.

At any rate, you can top off this walk by a tour of the new Twelfth District Federal Reserve Bank building right across the street at 101 Market. It's big, it's imposing, and it's filled with money—the vaults are down below.

The enormous lobby has a self-guided tour, "The World of Money" that offers exhibits and interactive computer games to teach you about banking and economics. There are different paths you can take through the exhibit depending upon your interests. Much of the material is devoted to telling you how important the Federal Reserve System is. This is not the place for anarchists.

GETTING BACK

To return, simply walk to the end of Market and cross the Embarcadero back to the Ferry building.

Looking east at the entrance to the Federal Reserve Bank on Market

Walking on Air—Rooftop Gardens WALK 5

San Francisco has several little-known rooftop gardens right in the downtown area. These sun terraces have been provided by the building owners for the people of San Francisco. They want you to come in and enjoy the flowers, the air, and the city views.

This walk provides a tour of three rooftop gardens. You can explore all three, pick your favorite, and then return many times later with a book, a friend, a brown-bag lunch, or all three to get a respite from the pressures of the working day.[1]

WALKING TIME

About 40 minutes. Note that this is *horizontal* walking only. It does not include the time getting up and down to and from the gardens.

GETTING THERE

From the Ferry Building, cross the Embarcadero and walk on the south side of Market Street until you come to the entrance of One Market Plaza, a block-sized building which is actually composed of three separate structures, the red brick fortress Southern Pacific building and two sleek new towers at Spear and Steuart.

Enter. This is not where the first rooftop garden is, but I want you to take a quick detour to look up at the astonishing skylight dome eleven stories above you. Under the skylight is a 131-foot-high latticed pavilion made of white aluminum panels. Many glittering San Francisco parties and special events are held right here, including a cocktail reception for the Black and White Ball.

---

[1] There are two other rooftop gardens in the Crocker Galleria, which I discuss in "Walk 14."

The now glamorous Southern Pacific Building is actually the approximate site of one of the bloodier episodes in San Francisco's history. On July 22, 1916, during a Preparedness Day parade (as in "prepare for war,") a pipe bomb exploded, killing 10 people and wounding 40. The city's union leaders were blamed, and labor activists Tom Mooney and Warren Billings were quickly tried, convicted, and sentenced—Mooney to death and Billings to life in prison. Many felt they were victims of Wild West justice and antiunion sentiment, and the two were often called the Sacco

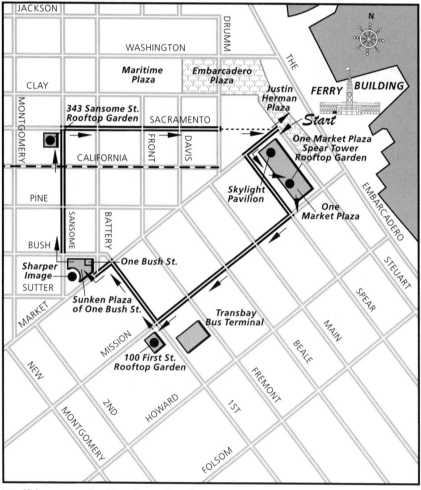

Walking on Air: Rooftop Gardens

and Venzetti of the West. After a 23-year international struggle, Mooney was finally pardoned in 1939, and Billings' sentence was commuted to time served. Billings did not receive an official pardon until 1961.

Now return to Market and continue to Spear Street. Turn left. About half-way down the block, you will come to the One Market Plaza address again. Enter. You are in One Market Plaza's Spear Street Tower. (Alternately, you can walk under the skylight and turn right into Spear Street Tower without going back outside.)

SPEAR TOWER AT ONE MARKET PLAZA

Take the elevator up to the seventh floor, and walk out to the rooftop garden. You will see a large circular grassy area surrounded by tables and chairs. The day I was there—early June—begonias were blooming away,

You are standing just a little below the Ferry Building clock, and the view of the Bay Bridge and the Ferry Building is as good as it gets. Through a window, you can see the lacy aluminum pavilion, still rising to its final height.

View of the Ferry Building from the rooftop garden at Spear Tower

ONE HUNDRED FIRST STREET

When you've had your fill of the views, take the elevator back down and exit Spear Tower. Walk south on Spear to Mission. Cross Mission, turn right and continue past the Transbay Bus Terminal, which you will see on your left. Cross First and walk left to 100 First Street.

This is not truly a "rooftop garden," because it's only one flight up! But it is included here because it is so inviting and lush. Simply take the escalator up, turn left past the elevators, and turn left again.

This garden is really set up for visitors. Little silvery tables and chairs are placed about invitingly. Petunias, agapanthus, and bird of paradise bloom among the potted palms. Long, grass-lined white cement benches invite snoozers, and on the day I was there, a man in business suit and tie was stretched out, oblivious to the world. A large rippled-glass fountain reflects the sunlight. Naturally, here is no view because you're not high enough, but you do feel that you're in a very special, tucked-away place.

343 SANSOME STREET

After you leave 100 First, walk north and cross Market at Battery. Turn left on Market. Just before you get to the small round Sharper Image building (532 Market), you will see some steps. Walk down to take a detour through the sunken plaza of One Bush Street. This is obviously not a rooftop garden—in fact, you're below street level—but it is an outdoor space where people gather, relax, chat, have lunch, and enjoy the large splashing fountain designed by David Tolerton. One problem is that there are no benches here, so you have to sit on the ground, which is hard on business clothes.

Walk through the plaza and exit on Bush. Turn left to cross Sansome, and then turn right on Sansome. Between California and Sacramento, you will come to the 343 Sansome building. Designed by John Galen Howard, the original building was constructed in 1908, with major add-ons in 1929 and 1990. Take the elevator up to the fifteenth floor. You know the building owners want you here because an elevator sign directs you to "Roof Garden on 15."

This sun terrace offers plenty of views, including an impressive one of the Transamerica Pyramid. The owners provide black metal tables and chairs as well as circular wooden benches with sitting pads on them. You can relax amongst the potted olive trees, petunias, bougainvillea, lobelia, and rosemary and look at the sculpture *Four Seasons Obelisk* by Joan Brown. A native San Francisco artist, Joan Brown died tragically in India in 1990 when the floor above her collapsed as she was installing one of her sculptures.

GETTING BACK

Leave the building via the Sacramento Street exit. But before you do, look at the fountain/sculpture in the lobby. This stainless steel water sculpture titled *L'Octagon* was constructed by French artist Pol Bury. Notice that those giant black balls *move*.

On Sacramento, head straight east back to the Ferry building.

The Four Seasons obelisk by Joan Brown in the rooftop garden at 343 Sansome

Sculpture Tour to Old Jackson Street

Old Jackson Street is part of the Jackson Square Historical District, which is bounded by Columbus, Pacific, Sansome, and Washington streets. First of all, it's not a square. It's not even a rectangle. It should properly be called Jackson Trapezoid Historical District, but I guess that's not very catchy.

Old Jackson's claim to fame is that it didn't tumble down during the '06 quake. Thus, as you walk through Jackson's 400 block, you see the pretty old brick buildings that have been standing since Gold Rush days. Why didn't they fall down? I'd always thought that brick structures on land fill would be the most vulnerable. But there they are. My husband Pete has pointed out the rows of large bolts on many of the buildings, which he theorizes "hold the building together," so maybe that's the reason.

Today, these buildings—beautifully restored—house elegant and expensive antique shops.

Even though old Jackson is closer to the Banker's Heart than to the Ferry Building, start from the Ferry Building, so you can enjoy the fine outdoor sculpture that lines your way as you walk. This route to Jackson Street is an outdoor sculpture garden. It's a museum in the streets.

WALKING TIME

About 45 minutes.

GETTING THERE: THE SCULPTURE TOUR

From the Ferry Building, cross the Embarcadero and walk into Justin Herman Plaza. Walk past the *Vaillancourt Fountain*, and turn left into Clay Street. At the northwest corner of Clay and Drumm, follow the zigzag path that leads up into Maritime Plaza and the Golden Gateway

*Movement the First 100 Years celebrates
100 years of U.S.-Korean diplomatic relations*

complex. You will quickly come upon steps that lead to a large abstract sculpture (often with bicycles leaning on it) called *Movement the First 100 Years*, celebrating 100 years of diplomatic relations—not all so peaceful—between Korea and the United States.

To the left are more steps and a walkway, which are a favorite practice ground for wild skateboarders, so look before you tread. Continue up.

Here on a platform in the air is a crisp, nautical city within a city, composed of Maritime Plaza and the Golden Gateway Center, a complex of high-rise apartments and townhouses. Continue around the Dean Witter Reynolds Building. You will be standing directly in front of dark, imposing One Maritime Plaza with its black exoskeleton. In front of you is a peacock-tail fountain, to your left, the sculpture *Limits of Horizon II* by

The fountain at One Maritime Plaza looks like a peacock tail

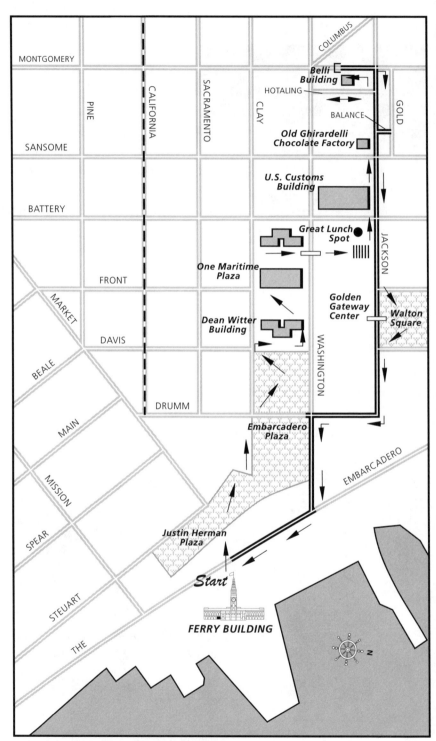

Sculpture Tour to Old Jackson Street

Jan Peter Stern, to your right Marino Marini's *Bronze Horse*. After viewing the sculptures, walk around the building. At the back, to the left, you can view Charles Perry's *Icosaspirale*, which looks kind of like a giant top or *dreidel*. On your right is the art collection's pièce de résistance, *Standing Figure Knife Edged* by Henry Moore.

Past this sculpture, turn right into the heart of the Golden Gateway complex. Signs direct you to places with crispy, seafaring names like Ironship Plaza, Whaleship Plaza, and Buckelew House. You will soon come upon a pond with a sculpture by Jacques Overhoff honoring the signing of the UN Charter.

Past the pond/sculpture descend the steps down to street level. You will be on Jackson. Turn left. At the corner of Jackson and Battery is a great brown-bag lunch spot—benches, cobblestones, and Seymour Lipton's sculpture *Pacific Bird*.

Cross Battery at Jackson to view the gigantic, newly restored U.S. Custom House (555 Battery). This is a *real* Custom House, not something out of a Dickens novel. If the customs inspectors at the airport think your bag of marjoram is really something else, it may be taken to the Custom House to be examined. (Maybe you will be too.) Take time to explore this high-ceilinged, airy, palatial building with its gleaming white staircases of Carrara marble. On the second floor, enter the room marked "U.S. Customs Entry Control" and look up at the ceiling to view the brilliantly colored friezes by A. Lincoln Cooper.

Continue on Jackson. Between Sansome and Montgomery is Jackson's historic 400 block.

OLD JACKSON STREET

This block, with its gingko and laurel trees and its comely red brick buildings is a welcome rest from the high-rises looming all around. For a moment, you can almost imagine you are back in Gold Rush days. On the north side of the street, the buildings date from the 1850s and are somewhat simpler in design. On the south side of the street, the buildings date from the 1860s and are quite a bit fancier, with lots of Victorian flourishes.

Here are the city's finest antique shops. Even if you don't go inside, you can peer through the windows at the objects—statues, Victorian furniture, oriental carpets. None of this stuff would exactly fit in my modest California bungalow, but I do enjoy looking!

Be sure to look at 415–35 Jackson, the unmarked site of Domingo Ghirardelli's old chocolate factory. Cutting into the north side of Jackson is tiny Balance Street, suppos-

Antique shop on Old Jackson Street

edly named for the ship *Balance*, buried below your feet. I looked very carefully but didn't see any masts poking up through the pavement. However, by 1849 there were 700 deserted ships in San Francisco Bay,[2] some of which became Bay fill, so it's very possible you *are* standing on a ship.

Another tiny street worth exploring is Hotaling, which cuts into the south side of the block. Notice the hitching posts at the entrance. As you walk down this alley with its wavy stone pavement, look at the marble lintel over the doorway of 27 Hotaling showing a woman holding wheat sheaves and poppies. Inside is Villa Taverna, a very private dining club. Don't go in.

On the sides of Hotaling are three fancy Italianate commercial build-ings (445, 451-55, and 463-73 Jackson) built in the 1860s and used as offices by businessman Anson Parsons Hotaling. Today they are occupied by elegant antique, art, and furniture shops.

On the corner of Jackson and Montgomery (498 Jackson) is the old Bank of Lucas, Turner & Co., built in 1853. Today a California

---

[2] Samuel Dickson. *San Francisco Kaleidoscope* in *Tales of San Francisco* (Stanford: Stanford University Press, 1949), p.386.

Registered Landmark, this bank is known as the "Sherman" bank after its first manager, William Tecumseh Sherman, who is better known for burning down Atlanta during the Civil War.

When you are through exploring old Jackson, take a left at Montgomery to view the Belli Building at 722 Montgomery and some other Gold-Rush-era survivors on the same block. Dating from 1851, the Belli building first housed a tobacco warehouse, then the Melodeon Theater, then, among other things, a Turkish bath. The late, well-known lawyer Melvin Belli bought this building and the adjacent Genella Building (728 Montgomery) and renovated both. The Genella Building once contained artist and writer studios on its upper floors, and supposedly Oscar Wilde visited here when he came to San Francisco in 1882.

Another oldie is the Golden Era Building (732 Montgomery), where the *Golden Era* literary magazine was published, offering writings by Mark Twain, Joaquin Miller, and Bret Harte.

GETTING BACK: MORE SCULPTURE

Start walking back on Jackson—remember every street has two sides.

When you get to Front, you will come upon Sydney G. Walton Square, between Pacific and Jackson. And herein lies a whole new sculpture garden. One of the most used patches of greenery in the city, this park is *filled* at lunchtime with workers brown-bagging and snoozing on the grass. In addition to people-viewing, you can view lots of art here, from the austere cast bronze *Portrait of Georgia O'Keefe* by Marisol to the playful *Big Heart on the Rock* by Jim Dine. And then there's the giant kinetic kitchen appliance *Two Open Rectangles* by George Rickey and *Pine Tree Obelisk* by the late San Francisco artist Joan Brown.[3] And, of course, the spurting *Fountain of Four Seasons* by Frenchman Francois Stahly. Take time and explore it all.

Now, walk to the southeast corner of the park and look across Jackson to see Benny Bufano's *The Penguins*. This is the last statue on my official tour.

---

[3] If you took "Walk 3" or "Walk 5" and enjoyed the Joan Brown obelisks, here is your chance to see another one.

While you're looking, ponder this mystery. Why is the Safeway across the street pretending to be a store called Bon Appétit? Is prosaic Safeway considered too low-class for this exalted neighborhood?

If you want to visit some of the sculptures again, climb the steps that lead straight up from Sydney G. Walton Square back into the Golden Gateway complex. You can't get lost as you wander around because the Ferry Building will be visible on your left.

Otherwise, continue down Jackson to Drumm. Turn right on Drumm and continue until you cross Washington, where you have both a traffic light and a crosswalk, so you can cross the busy Embarcadero safely. Cross and continue south back to the Ferry Building.

Pier Walk South

This is a walk that would not exist if the Embarcadero Freeway had not been torn down after the Loma Prieta earthquake. That is, the walk would exist but no one would go on it. Now, however, you can mingle with other eager strollers, joggers, bikers, skaters, fishermen, artists, skateboarders, and with the ubiquitous homeless—all taking in the air and views of San Francisco's reborn waterfront.

The waterfront promenade—from China Basin to Fisherman's Wharf—is now called Herb Caen Way, sometimes written "Herb Caen Way...".

Note that the entire San Francisco waterfront is undergoing renovation, so what I write here may not be accurate in a few years. Ten years ago, if I had described the Embarcadero without a freeway and lined with elegant palm trees, readers would have assumed I had been ingesting a hallucinogenic substance, but that's exactly how the Embarcadero does look today.

As you walk, remember that the entire Embarcadero is built on fill, some of which consists of abandoned Gold-Rush-era sailing vessels. So, you're walking on ghosts.

WALKING TIME

A little over an hour. This is steady walking—long blocks and few traffic lights.

GETTING THERE

Like Gertrude Stein said about Oakland, "There is no there there." The walk, itself, is the goal, so make sure to look around you as you go and savor every moment. The grandeur of the Bay Bridge dominates. As

View of the Bay Bridge and Yerba Buena Island from Herb Caen Way

you stroll, you will experience it from many inspiring angles and vantage points—even from directly underneath!

THE PIERS

From the Ferry Building head south along the Embarcadero. Just past Mission, the promenade opens up, so you can walk right at the water's edge and view the bobbing sailboats. The occasional fisherman will be dropping a line into the Bay, fishing for perch. I have never seen anyone catch anything here. I'm not saying people don't; I'm just saying I've never seen it.

You will pass a plaque honoring the American Merchant Seamen who died in Vietnam.

Just before Harrison, the walk pulls away from the water and the area gets, well, a little grungy. This less glamorous section has the feel of a working waterfront, so it's interesting too. Cafés—little more than shacks—with names like "The Boondocks Restaurant" and "Red's Java House" add to the nautical feel. Along the walk, black and white pillars (zebra poles) provide information about the waterfront's history.

Starting at Harrison, you will see a running concrete structure that contains a ribbon of glass brick. It doesn't look like much during the day, but at night the bricks are illuminated, creating a striking ribbon of light that keeps pace with you as you walk.

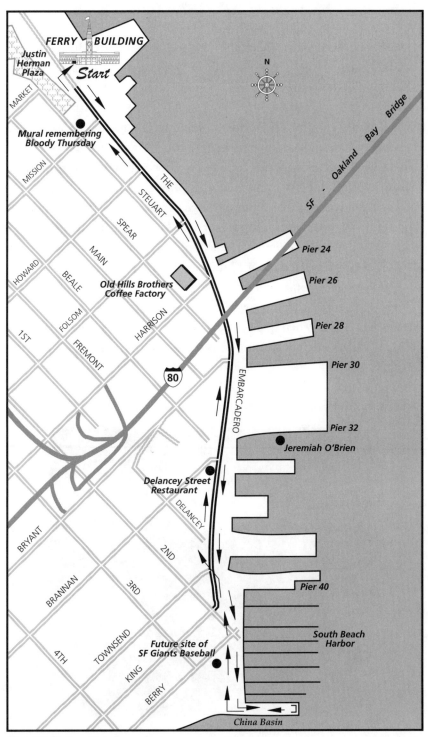

Pier Walk South

Past Harrison, cross under the Bridge. Look up and hope that its 200,000 tons of steel stay where they're supposed to, at least until you safely pass underneath.

At Pier 32, you will pass the SS *Jeremiah O'Brien*, the crusty old World War II vessel that in 1994 made an historic five-month voyage to the beaches of Normandy to commemorate the 50th anniversary of D-Day. This ship is one of only two fully restored operating survivors of 2,710 World War II Liberty ships and the only ship participating in the Normandy invasions that returned 50 years later for the anniversary. On this return voyage, the old ship was crewed by volunteers, many of whom were World War II veterans. The skipper, 78-year old Captain George Jahn, was captain of a different Liberty ship on D-Day.

The *Jeremiah O'Brien* made the 1998 Oscars! The engine room of the *Titanic* in the in Academy-Award film is really the engine room of the *Jeremiah O'Brien*. When spellbound moviegoers watch the dramatic scene of the *Titanic's* engines shifting into reverse after the ship hits a North Atlantic iceberg, they are actually watching the *Jeremiah O'Brien's* engines as the ship sails on the Bay! The pounding that won the Academy Award for Best Sound is the pounding of the *Jeremiah O'Brien's* engines.

The Jeremiah O'Brien at Pier 32

South Beach Marina

The *Jeremiah O'Brien* is open for visitors. There is a modest admission charge.

Past Pier 40, where you can charter boats, you come upon the glamorous South Beach Harbor and Marina. Here is open space, mounds of bougainvillea and roses, a ship—the *Dolphin P. Rempp*— dragged ashore to become a trendy restaurant, picnic spots, a harbor office, and dock after dock of sailboats. There are also phones and clean, free restrooms.

At this Marina, I always find the usual San Francisco mixture of cultures: picnicking immigrant families, wealthy boat owners, a gentleman talking on his cellular phone and leaning on a dumpster with its warning sign "KEEP OUT OF DUMPSTERS."

Continue past Dock G to a pedestrian pier that extends into the Bay. Walk out, past the fountain for fish cleaning and past the silent fishermen. At the end, you will come to a circular bench. This is the place to view the Bridge and eat your sandwich.

GETTING BACK

Depending upon your mood, you can continue back the way you came and stay near the water, or you can cross the Embarcadero and look at some of South of Market's fancy new neighborhoods. Or you can mix the two, and cross back and forth as the mood strikes.

To view the neighborhoods, cross the Embarcadero at Townsend. Note how attractive the residences are with their landscaped exteriors.

A sign tells you the history of Rincon Hill, which you can see as you look west. It explains why the hill, once 120 feet high, today looks more like Rincon "mound." It's because the hill was shaved to accommodate the Bay Bridge anchorage.

Between Townsend and Brannan, you will come to an attractive Mission-style structure, the headquarters of the Delancey Street Foundation, a drug and alcohol rehabilitation center founded by the late John Maher and criminologist Mimi Silbert. The Delancey Street Foundation runs a number of businesses to promote its concepts of responsibility and self-sufficiency, including a moving company, an inline skate rental, a print shop, and a car repair shop. At the corner of Embarcadero and Brannan, you will also see the elegant Delancey Street Restaurant, with its outdoor seating and valet parking.

The headquarters building itself was largely constructed by the ex-criminals and addicts in the Delancey Street program.

As you walk, you will see bronze plaques in the sidewalk that, like the zebra poles on the water side of the Embarcadero, illuminate the history of the area. They're interesting, but they take a while to read.

Just south of Folsom, is the red brick Hills Brothers complex. This collection of shops and businesses is the site of the old Hills Brothers Coffee factory, where in 1890 this company revolutionized the coffee industry by vacuum-packing roasted ground coffee in sealed tins. Although the facade has been refurbished, the dominating Hills Brothers roof-top sign is original. Walk up the steps to look at the fountain.

Continue to Mission. At Mission and Steuart, notice the large mural and plaque in memory of the men who died on "Bloody Thursday," July 5, 1934, during the San Francisco Longshoremen's strike. Although we hear little about this strike today, at the time, it was considered nothing less than a civil war. The Daily News of July 6, 1934, reported: "Among the no-man's-land of the Embarcadero and the far-flung area from

Market St. to Rincon Hill, on up to Second St., the battles raged. Yesterday's war of the streets had for its Bunker Hill the battle of Rincon Hill, its terrors for hundreds of curious spectators the seize of the Ferry Building, the attack on the trains...." So, the serene area you've just walked through wasn't always so peaceful.

Continue back to the Ferry Building.

The Old Warehouse District & Levi's Plaza

San Francisco's warehouse district nestles on what once was the edge of the city, clustering around Front, Battery, and Sansome streets Here companies such as Armour Packing Company, American Biscuit Company, and Petri-Italian-American Cigar Company stored their wares and conducted business. Most of the massive old buildings are built of red brick; a few of reinforced concrete. A great number date from 1907, the year following the great earthquake and fire.

Today, with almost all shipping going through the Port of Oakland, many of San Francisco's warehouses have been converted to showrooms and offices. Others have "Available" signs posted in front.

In the center of the district is Levi's Plaza, a four-acre complex which contains the Levi Strauss & Company headquarters, fountains, open space, kiosks with public phones and shaded benches, a restaurant, and a little park. Built in 1982, the complex was designed to fit in with the surrounding warehouse district. And it does.

WALKING TIME

Allow at least an hour and a half.

GETTING THERE

From the Ferry Building, cross over to Justin Herman Plaza, and then cut through Justin Herman and Embarcadero plazas to Washington Street. Continue north on Drumm. The Golden Gateway Tennis & Swim Club will be on your right, and, after you cross Jackson, the Golden Gateway Commons on your left.

The Club is blocked by a high fence, so you can't see much, but you can hear the thunk, thunk of the tennis balls as you walk along. The Commons is a collection of rosy-colored little townhouses and condos,

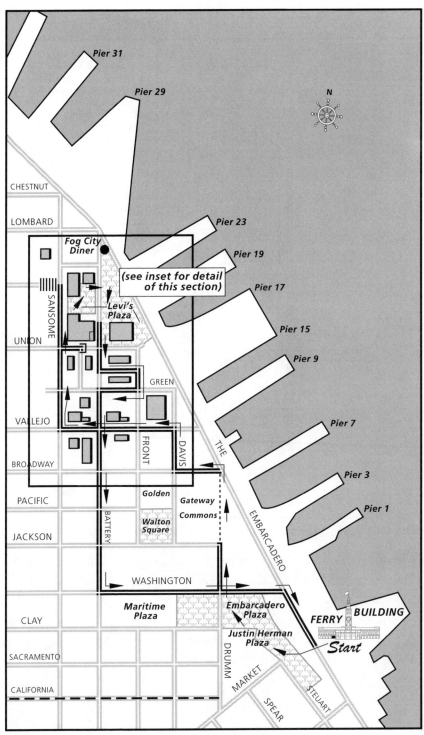

The Old Warehouse District and Levi's Plaza

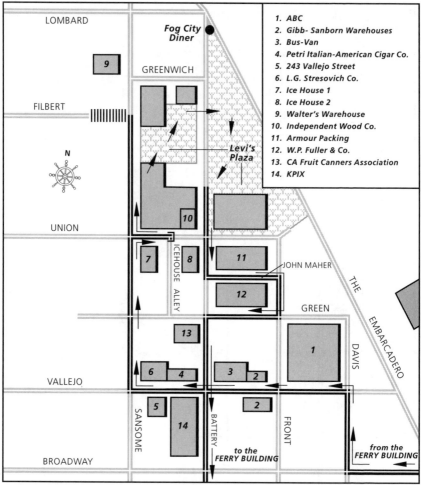

The Old Warehouse District and Levi's Plaza (inset)

whose geometric outlines always remind me of a fort. Past Jackson, Drumm becomes a footpath through the condos, so you walk without traffic.

The Drumm path ends at Broadway. Turn left on Broadway and walk one block to Davis. Then, turn right on Davis to Vallejo. Walk west on Vallejo to Front. To your right is the ABC television studio.

WAREHOUSES

At Front, Vallejo is sandwiched between the two large Gibb-Sanborn warehouses (855 and 915 Front). Originally built about 1855, these are the district's oldest buildings. They partially burned in 1906 and were rebuilt exactly as they had been. If you examine the bricks, you can see different shades of red from the different eras.

On the northwest corner of Battery and Vallejo is another giant, the Petri Italian-American Cigar Company at 901 Battery. (And on the northeast corner, Busvan for Bargains, where I bought my meager furnishings when I first arrived in San Francisco in 1965).

Continue uphill on Vallejo. Notice the pretty bright blue building at 243 Vallejo. Built in 1930, the structure has decorative designs molded right into the stucco. The little white brick building to its right dates from 1906.

At Sansome turn right. You will be in front of the great gray L.G. Sresovich Company warehouse (1000 Sansome), which was originally built in 1892 to contain fruit. The original decorative molding of grape vines is still over the doorway. The structure was rebuilt in 1906 for the

The Gold-Rush era Gibb-Sanborn warehouse at 915 Front

Bemis Bag Company, which also owned warehouses at 1050 and 1090 Sansome.

At Green, look to your left to see the dramatic rugged east slope of Telegraph Hill. In the early 20th century, the Gray Brothers quarried rock from this slope until houses started tumbling down. Finally, someone killed George Gray and that put an effective damper on the quarrying operation. More recently, winter storms and erosion have caused further changes to this steep, rocky outcropping.

The rugged east slope of Telegraph Hill, and a humorous sign

At Union, you can detour down the steps on your right to look at the two Ice House warehouses on Ice House Lane. Built in 1914 for National Ice & Cold Storage, the buildings were made into interior decorator showrooms in 1970. Today they are part of the Levi Strauss & Company headquarters.

At Filbert, look to your left to view the Filbert steps and also the Walters Warehouse (1301 Sansome), which today has a house, garden, and guesthouse, all on the roof. Then, turn right into Levi's Plaza.

LEVI'S PLAZA

What a great place to eat lunch. The company calls Levi's Plaza a "campus," and, for a visitor, it is like a campus—minus the stress and hurry. This inviting open space was created for the public, so Levi Strauss wants you to be here.

Levi's has a long history in this city. (That little "S.F." on the Levi's rivets stands for "San Francisco.") The firm actually dates from 1853 when the Bavarian peddler Levi Strauss joined his brother-in-law, clothing importer David Stern, in San Francisco. When gold miners complained that their work pants were falling apart, Levi Strauss started producing sturdy denim pants, held together by tough seams and copper rivets. The rest is history. "Dungarees" we used to call these tough pants when I was a kid. Then just "jeans," And finally "Levi's," as though there simply weren't any other kind.

Managed today by the Haas family, Levi Strauss & Company regularly appears on lists of the best places to work in the United States.

The red brick of the complex's buildings blends in gently with its warehouse neighborhood. One of the buildings is actually not new at all. This is the Italian Swiss Colony wine warehouse at Battery and Greenwich, which was built in 1903. Once a cooperative for unemployed Italian immigrants, then later a storage facility for wine, the building today contains an Il Fornaio Restaurant and offices.

The landscape architect Lawrence Halprin designed the appealing Plaza grounds, which are bordered by Sansome, Greenwich, Union, and the Embarcadero. The granite fountain offers many tempting places to sit. As at the *Vaillancourt Fountain*, you can walk under and through the structure on steps and concrete blocks, getting as wet as you want.

Enter the headquarters building to look at an historic display about Levi's jeans. My favorite object here is the sculpture *Blue Levi Jacket* by Frank Duchamp. At first, you won't see any sculpture; you'll just see a jacket on a hanger. But that jacket is actually a wood sculpture. This is real *trompe l'oeil*.

You can also stroll through the park on the east side of Battery, with its miniature hills and dales, stream, stone benches, curvy paths, and a second fountain. The park is landscaped to obscure traffic from its eastern boundary, the Embarcadero. This area is a little too artificial for my taste, so I usually sit in the main part of the Plaza for my people watching.

At the corner of Battery and the Embarcadero is the Fog City Diner. But don't expect to drop in here for a quick burger and fries. This glitzy neon and chrome eatery is the kind of diner where you need to make reservations.

MORE WAREHOUSES

When you're through enjoying the Plaza, start back along Battery. At 1105 Battery is the Independent Wood Company building. Incredibly picturesque, this little 1907 brick building once provided lodging for sailors.

Cross Union and you will be at my favorite block in the district. This entire block consists of mammoth red brick warehouses. At 1050 Battery is the Armour Packing Company smokehouse. Turn down Union a little way to explore the sides of this building and also 55 Union to look at the brick decorations on the side. Then return to Battery.

My favorite warehouse on my favorite block is the W.P. Fuller & Company building at 1010 Battery (also 50 Green, 60 Green, and 1001 Front). Walk down gray brick John Maher Alley to Front to view the building's gigantic arches from all sides. Designed by architects G.A. Wright and Willis Polk and completed in 1907, this building was used by Fuller & Company for glass and mirrors, and the arches were made large enough for railroad cars to roll through. At Front, look through the giant arches into the structure itself. Today it houses Landor Associates, a design consulting firm.

In Front Street, directly east of John Maher Alley, you can see some of the 1907 tracks from the Belt Line Railroad, which once hauled merchandise from the ships that sailed into San Francisco's port.

On Front, walk to Green and turn right to return to Battery. As you walk, you can see more old track and also the fourth side of the remarkable W.P. Fuller & Company warehouse.

On the southwest corner of Battery and Green (945 Battery) is an ancient-looking warehouse with a sign on the door warning you that the building is made of unreinforced masonry and might be unsafe during a quake. Once the California Fruit Canners Association warehouse, today this warehouse holds Levi's jeans. If you cross Green again and back up a little way toward Levi's Plaza, you can look toward the warehouse and see it contrast startlingly with the Transamerica Pyramid rising behind it.

At 901 Battery, you can get another view of the Petri Italian-American Cigar Company warehouse, and then, across Vallejo, at 875 Battery, the reinforced concrete American Biscuit Company building built in 1907. Today, the whole block from Vallejo to Broadway on the west side of Battery is taken over by the KPIX television studios.

GETTING BACK

Continue on Battery to Washington. Then turn left and continue on Washington until you cross the Embarcadero. Turn south to return to the Ferry Building.

Pier Walk North

This is a really long walk so allow plenty of time. The trail curves along the Embarcadero with spectacular views of downtown, the warehouse district, and Telegraph Hill. You will pass through the heart of San Francisco's tourist mecca, and then out onto the Municipal Pier for a quiet view of the Bay.

As you walk, remember that the entire waterfront is being renovated, so where I describe an old pier, you may find a shop, a luxury hotel, or, simply, a welcome open space.

WALKING TIME
Two and a half hours, straight walking.

GETTING THERE
Like the "Walk 7: Pier Walk South," you are already there, enjoying a vista created by the demolition of the Embarcadero Freeway.

THE PIERS
From the Ferry Building, head north on the Embarcadero Promenade, now called Herb Caen Way. You will share the path with a mix of strollers, joggers, bikers, skaters, and skateboarders. In the early part of this walk, the Bay will be obscured by wharf buildings much of the time, with only occasional openings onto the water. However, you will be more than compensated by the magnificent panorama of San Francisco that rises to the west.

Look across the Embarcadero to see the full sweep of the San Francisco skyline: the massive Bank of America building, the many-layered Hyatt Regency, the Embarcadero towers, the dark, exoskeletal Alcoa building with the Transamerica Pyramid climbing behind it. Past

Washington, you can see the sharp geometric outlines of the red Golden Gateway Commons condos with Coit Tower peeping up behind them.

Right before the entrance to Pier 7 (see "Walk 2"), the ribbon of glass brick begins. (Eventually, this "Art Ribbon" project will stretch from Fisherman's Wharf to China Basin.) At night, the ribbon is lit and outlines the San Francisco shoreline. Here, also you can see palm trees where the freeway once was, elegant Victorian lampposts, and what I call "zebra poles"—black and white pillars that provide you with historical information as you walk along. Look at the little working tugs moored at Pier 15.

Then look the other way, at the fabulous view of the red brick warehouse district to your west. You can see the sign Landor Associates on the old W.P. Fuller & Company warehouse. As you continue, make sure to also look at the rugged east slope of Telegraph Hill.

At Pier 23 is a little lunch shack, crowded with diners; on the other side of the Embarcadero, the trendy Fog City Diner. If you haven't made reservations, you'd better stick to the little shack at Pier 23.

After Lombard, the Embarcadero curves sharply west, and soon you will come to Sydney Rudy Waterfront Park, which continues from Pier 35 all the way to Pier 39. Here you *can* see the Bay. In fact, there are observation decks to help you. Walk along the boardwalk and enjoy the flowers, the topiary (leafy reindeer, dolphins, crabs, and octopus), the nautical air, the shiny sculpture *Skygate* by Roger Barr, or just watch the sailboats slicing through the water.

At Pier 39, the crowds thicken (see "Walk 21"). You can stop here for a snack or press on. At Pier 41 are plenty of benches if you want to rest. Walk out a way on this pier. You can see the famous Pier 39 sea lions from here and also enjoy the comings and goings of the Red and White Fleet ferries. Best of all is the view of Alcatraz.

At Pier 43 is a strange-looking arch with even stranger-looking, very ancient tracks running out of it toward the water, where they suddenly stop. This is the Ferry Arch. Ferries carrying railroad cars used to dock here. Then, the railcars would roll right off of the ferries onto the tracks, and from there to their connection points. The large bulkhead arch is

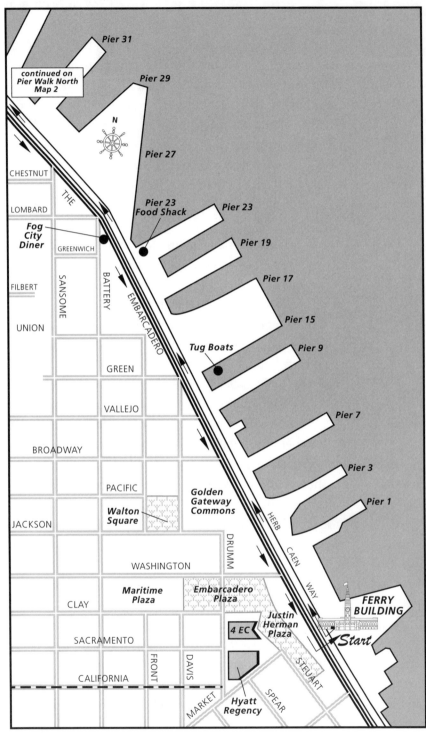

continued on
Pier Walk North
Map 2

Pier 31

Pier 29

N

Pier 27

CHESTNUT

LOMBARD

THE

*Fog
City
Diner*

GREENWICH

Pier 23
Food Shack

Pier 23

Pier 19

FILBERT

SANSOME

BATTERY

EMBARCADERO

Pier 17

UNION

Pier 15

GREEN

Tug Boats

Pier 9

VALLEJO

Pier 7

BROADWAY

PACIFIC

*Golden
Gateway
Commons*

Pier 3

*Walton
Square*

Pier 1

JACKSON

DRUMM

WASHINGTON

HERB

CAEN

WAY

Maritime
Plaza

Embarcadero
Plaza

CLAY

Justin
Herman
Plaza

FERRY
BUILDING

SACRAMENTO

4 EC

Start

STEUART

CALIFORNIA

FRONT

DAVIS

SPEAR

MARKET

*Hyatt
Regency*

Pier Walk North - Map 1

The Ferry Arch at Pier 43, where once railroad cars rolled off the ferries right onto railroad tracks

just decorative, a Beaux Arts remnant of San Francisco's City Beautiful movement early in the century.

You are now in Fisherman's Wharf, which has no exact beginning or end. Originally, it referred to the dock area between Taylor and Leavenworth, where Italian American fishermen once actually set sail to fish, but today the term blankets everything from Pier 39 to the Municipal Pier at Van Ness. Since World War II, the whole waterfront area has become primarily a gigantic tourist attraction with a fishing motif. There are, however, some genuine fishermen still here, and if you want to get up at 4 A.M., you can see them bring in their catch. (Today, most of the fish served in the Wharf restaurants arrive by truck, not by boat.) If you don't want to get up so early, you can get the "Fisherman's Wharf" feel by walking over to one of the outdoor fish stalls at Jefferson and Taylor and buying a cracked crab cocktail.

Gigantic Pier 45 with its long sheds is one of the true remaining working piers. Before dawn, commercial fishermen labor in the soupy fog to unload their catches of salmon, bass, and herring. On the east side of the

The Fisherman's & Seaman's Chapel at Pier 45

Pier is the USS *Pampanito*, a World War II submarine. Touring the ship costs money, but you can pick up an informational pamphlet for free.

Pier 45 is the Wharf's longest pier, and if you walk to the end, you will be rewarded with spectacular views. At the entrance to the Pier, on the west end, is the Fisherman's Grotto restaurant. If you enter the Pier and walk past the long north edge of the restaurant, you will come to a tiny chapel across from Shed B. This is the Fisherman's & Seaman's Chapel, which honors San Francisco's fishermen, especially those who have died at sea. The Chapel holds Roman Catholic Mass on Sunday mornings.

Now, turn down Taylor and walk along Jefferson to get a feel of the "tourist" Wharf. The streets are often so crowded that you will just inch along. Here are the simmering crab pots, the street vendors, the sketch artists, the shops—Sweet Fantasy, Crazy Shirts, Frank's Fisherman—selling candy, tee shirts, and souvenirs, and whatever else you can think of.

If you've had enough of the tourist attractions, return to the water at Jones to look at the fishing fleet. From here to Hyde are the "genuine" fishing boats that bring in the fish every morning. Of course, there are a lot of pleasure boats here too.

At Leavenworth, head south and cross Jefferson. You will be at the Cannery, a 1906 red brick building, where Del Monte once canned peaches. In 1968, this structure was reborn as a complex containing shops, restaurants, and a comedy club. Take the outdoor elevator to the third floor to look into the Museum of the City of San Francisco (free,

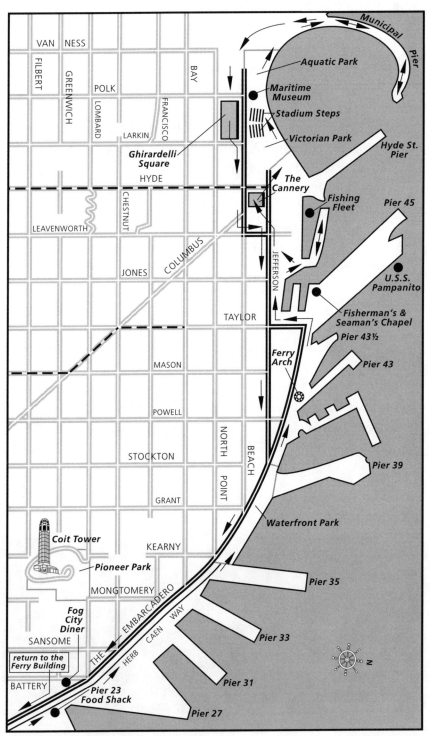

Pier Walk North - Map 2

open Wednesday through Sunday from 10 A.M. to 4 P.M.). The elevator ride provides a wonderful view of the Bay. The Museum is filled with San Francisco memorabilia, including Herb Caen's desk, (but not his type-writer; that's at the *Chronicle*).

Between the Cannery and the empty Haslett warehouse to the west is an inviting, shady courtyard, where you can rest on a bench and occa-sionally enjoy free entertainment.

Continue on Jefferson past the Hyde Street Pier. Once this pier ser-viced ferries carrying people to Sausalito and Berkeley. Today it is part of the National Park system and boasts a number of historic ships. You must pay, not just to explore the ships, but even to enter the pier, which I find extremely irritating.

Across Hyde Street, grassy Victorian Park and the cable car turn-around will be to your left, the South End Rowing Club and the Dolphin Swimming and Boating Club to your right. The water looks totally uninviting—cold and none too clean—but you will see children wading and possibly even a few hardy older folks swimming away.

There is a beach here with actual sand. Rumor has it that the sand was carted from underneath Union Square when it was excavated for the underground garage. Large concrete stadium steps face the water, but the only show is on the steps themselves, where drummers will entertain you as you walk along.

South of the steps, on the other side of Beach Street, is Ghirardelli Square, originally the site of Pioneer Woolen Mill, but more famous as

Tug boats at Pier 15

the site of the old Ghirardelli Chocolate Factory. From 1962 to 1967 this area was converted into today's complex of shops, galleries, and restaurants. The *Mermaid Fountain* in the center was designed by Ruth Asawa.

Continuing along the water, you will come to the Maritime Museum, which is housed in an Art Deco building that looks like a luxury liner. Built during the Depression by the WPA, the "ship" today houses artifacts, models of ships, and photographs that recount the city's maritime history. The museum is free and open daily from 10 A.M. to 5 P.M.

Directly west of the Museum's entrance, is a bocce ball court, where you can watch serious players at their daily games.

Continue along the water and follow the path onto the long, curved Municipal Pier, which extends 1,850 feet into the water. Unlike at Pier 7, there are no comfortable benches here, no Victorian lampposts—in fact no lights at all. The Municipal Pier is one unrelieved slab of concrete. But walk to the end; the view is worth it.

GETTING BACK

Go back the way you came, except walk inland a little way from the water to spend more time exploring Ghirardelli Square and the interior parts of the Fisherman's Wharf along Jefferson.

If you're just too tired to walk back, catch the 32 bus at Hyde and Beach. This will take you to back to the Ferry Building. You can also catch the 42 bus anywhere along North Point to return to the Embarcadero BART station, a few minutes' walk from the Ferry Building.

Gandhi looking ready to stroll across the Bay

The "Banker's Heart" sculpture, Bank of America World Headquarters, Kearny & California

If you're in the mood to get some fresh air, but not to do much actual walking, then St. Mary's Square is a perfect place to enjoy the San Francisco breezes and munch your sandwich.

If you're not in the mood to do much walking or get fresh air, you can enjoy a noontime concert at Old St. Mary's Cathedral across the street from the Square.

If you're feeling completely lazy, you can sit motionless at your desk and visit Old St. Mary's at its Web site at: http://members.aol.com/dovecsp/oldstmarys_sf . You can't hear the music though. At least not yet.

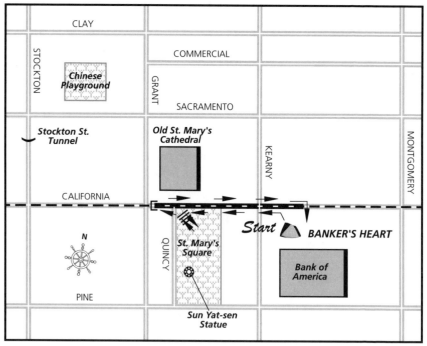

St. Mary's Square and Old St. Mary's Cathedral

WALKING TIME

Less than ten minutes round trip.

GETTING THERE

This is a miniwalk. From the Banker's Heart at Kearny and California, cross Kearny and start walking west up the hill. Just past St. Mary's Square garage, you will see some concrete steps. Walk up, and you will be in St. Mary's Square.

THE SQUARE

The little park is quiet and shady with comfortable benches. (If you think about it, though, you will realize that

Old St. Mary's Cathedral from St. Mary's Square

this urban oasis is actually the roof of the parking garage.)

In the morning, neighborhood denizens engage in a variety of forms of exercise in the park, but by lunchtime most of the serious activity has long ended. However, you can often see a lone Tai Chi-er or two executing the slow, graceful movements of this martial art.

On your right (toward Grant Avenue) is a huge steel and granite statue of Chinese revolutionary Dr. Sun Yat-sen, the first president of the Republic of China. Executed by sculptor Benny Bufano, the statue was commissioned as part of Roosevelt's Works Progress Administration (WPA) and placed in the park in 1938. Note particularly the gleaming steel cloak.

Dr. Sun Yat-sen actually lived in San Francisco from 1904 to about 1910, hiding from assassins and working to promote his democratic ideals in the Chinese community. He and Benny Bufano knew one another at this time.

The Bank of America building from St. Mary's Square

I'm explaining all this because when I showed the statue (from my office window) to one of the well-paid but poorly educated programmers who works with me, he said, "Who's Benny Bufano that Sun Yat-sen made a statue of him?"

After you view the statue, turn around to see the Bank of America building at its absolute best. Its massive bulk actually appears elegant and even graceful. You will also notice a unobtrusive bronze plaque that lists "these Americans of Chinese ancestry who gave their lives for America in World Wars I and II."

The little park boasts the rare distinction of having two toilet facilities. At the southwest corner is one of San Francisco's new, modern French toilets manufactured by JCDecaux. This glitzy green and gold toilet costs a quarter to use, and if you aren't out in 20 minutes, the door will open, to your eternal mortification. To the east (Kearny side), is an ordinary park toilet, humble but functional—at least the Ladies room is. The Men's room was boarded up at the time of writing.

THE CATHEDRAL

To get to Old St. Mary's Cathedral, leave the park the way you entered and cross California at Grant. Old St. Mary's offers live music to the downtown crowd on Tuesdays and Thursdays at 12:30. The concerts last a half-an-hour. You are asked to make a donation, but no one is turned away. (Just walk into the Cathedral to get a concert schedule for the upcoming month.)

Before you enter, notice the hodgepodge of architectural styles in which this pretty church sits. On the left (across Grant) is the Sing

Chong building with its green and red pagoda. To the right, past the parish house, is 650 California Street, a towering, cream-colored, ultra-modern office building. The cathedral, itself, is "Gothic Revival." If you cross California Street again and walk up the hill a bit, you can look back to see the Transamerica Pyramid added to the architectural soup.

Old St. Mary's sits in a mixture of architectural styles

Built by Chinese laborers in 1853 and '54, Old St. Mary's was the first Roman Catholic cathedral in California as well as the tallest building, although it looks tiny now. Constructed of granite shipped from China and New England brick transported around Cape Horn as ships' ballast, the sturdy church survived the 1906 earthquake, although the interior was gutted by the fire that followed.

In its early days, St. Mary's had its work cut out for it. Grant Avenue— then called Dupont Street—was home to a wild red-light district. In the 1890s, the irate citizens of San Francisco cleaned up Dupont, whereupon the brothels all moved to shacks lining St. Mary's Square. San Francisco memoirist Samuel Dickson reminisced:

> Tattoo artists and proprietors of shooting galleries opened shops. The sickly sweet odor of opium smoke drifted through the square.[4]

---

[4] Samuel Dickson. *San Francisco Kaleidoscope* in *Tales of San Francisco* (Stanford: Stanford University Press, 1949), p.519.

Perhaps this is why the ominous message from Ecclesiastes, "Son, observe the time and fly from evil," is carved into the church tower, staring sternly out at St. Mary's Square.

In 1891, a new St. Mary's Cathedral was completed at safer and more fashionable Van Ness and O'Farrell, and in 1994, the original cathedral officially became "Old St. Mary's," a parish church run by the Paulist Fathers, who minister to the nearby community. Today, this church still has its work cut out for it, judging by the number of homeless' carts that have replaced the brothels in the church neighborhood.

Although the inside of Old St. Mary's is not considered "noteworthy" because none of it is original, I found that the quiet, darkened, tranquil interior provided a needed respite from the bustle of the financial-district frenzy.

GETTING BACK

If you can't figure how to get back, you're in trouble.

Mini Museum Tour: Wells Fargo, Pacific Heritage, Chinese Historical Society of America

Within a block or two of the Banker's Heart are three tiny museums, each with a totally different feel and each providing you with a totally different take on life in the "West." All three are worthwhile and all three are free.

WALKING TIME
Less than 10 minutes round trip.

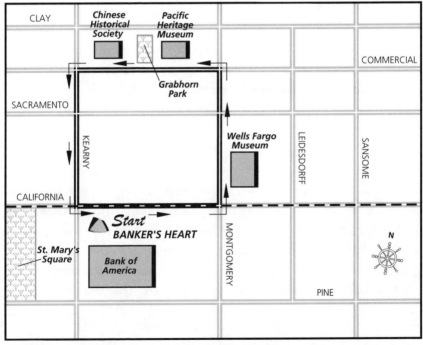

Mini Museum Tour: Wells Fargo, Pacific Heritage, Chinese Historical Society of America

GETTING THERE

The Wells Fargo History Museum is just a block from the Banker's Heart at Kearny and California. Simply walk east on California to Montgomery, cross Montgomery, turn left, and continue to the Museum at 420 Montgomery.

THE WELLS FARGO HISTORY MUSEUM

The museum is open Monday through Friday from 9 A.M. to 5 P.M.

Generally, bank history is not a topic that makes the heart go pitter-patter. What makes Wells Fargo different is its role in the San Francisco Gold Rush, its operation of cross-country stagecoaches, and, most exciting to me, its running of the Pony Express, which for 18 months transported mail between St. Louis, Missouri, and Sacramento, California at the "lightning" speed of 8 to 15 days. Wells Fargo took over operation of the Pony Express in April 1861 from the Central Overland California & Pikes Peak Express, which had advertised for "young, skinny, wiry fellows, not over 18. Must be expert riders, willing to risk death daily. Orphans preferred."[5]

On the main floor, you can see lots of Gold Rush history as well as a "real" 1868 stagecoach, or you can go through the elevator lobby to the actual Wells Fargo bank, where another authentic coach is on display. Notice the gigantic wheels, necessary for fording streams and keeping passengers safely above mud and brush.

On the Museum's upper floor you can sit in a stagecoach (not authentic), press a red button, and listen to the journal of Francis Brocklehurst's 2,700-mile overland stagecoach journey from St. Louis to San Francisco in the spring of 1859. Brocklehurst describes the streams forded and waded, the endless boiled beans consumed at a dollar a serving, and the alkaline dust that covered him on this no-bathing, month-long journey.

On the upper floor, you can also see a "mochila," a light saddle covering that held the actual mail in its four pockets. The young rider could

---

[5] Emmy E. Werner, *Pioneer Children on the Journey West* (Boulder: Westview Press, 1995), p. 152.

quickly slip the mochila over the new saddle whenever he changed to a fresh horse. Each mochila held a maximum of 20 pounds of mail, which, today, would hardly be enough to justify a cross-country run.

Most fascinating to me was the man behind the information desk, who told me about his great-grandparents' journey to California in a covered wagon in 1847, only a year after the Donner party's tragic trek. He, himself, was from Marysville, a town named for Donner-party survivor Mary Murphy.

This kindly guide pointed out the four and six dollar bills issued by eastern banks and the rare jewelry with veins of gold running through quartz.

THE PACIFIC HERITAGE MUSEUM

When you leave Wells Fargo, continue north on Montgomery to Commercial Street. It's hard to imagine now, but you are just about at San Francisco's original shoreline. If you had jumped off the curb (which wasn't there), you might have found yourself wading in the Bay. Cross Commercial and turn left.

Narrow Commercial Street was not part of the original little village laid out by Jean Jacques Vioget in 1839. Created in 1850, the street originally ran from Grant Avenue (then Dupont) to a wharf that extended into the Bay until about where Drumm Street is today. Commercial was home to many brick business buildings created to deal with commerce generated by the wharf. Later, the Grant end of Commercial (the 700 block) was also home to many brothels, so the street was "commercial" in more ways than one.

At 608 Commercial, you will come to the Pacific Heritage Museum (open Tuesday through Saturday 10 A.M. to 4 P.M.).

This building was the site of the first U.S. Branch Mint, which opened in 1854 to deal with the Gold Rush. When the Bank of Canton built its modern office building in 1984, it was required to leave this official landmark building intact. On the site, the Bank created the beautiful Pacific Heritage Museum and dedicated it to art and culture of the Pacific Rim. Thus, the Pacific Heritage Museum is actually two museums squashed into one—the old mint and the Pacific Rim.

Despite this odd marriage, the wonderful little museum is an oasis of peace. The calming music, open space, play of light and air, and magnificent exhibits create an atmosphere so transforming that you will not believe you are in the midst of San Francisco's frenetic financial district. The exhibition of contemporary Chinese calligraphy that I saw was worthy of being placed in any great museum.

On the lower floor, the "mint" museum takes precedence—with a vault area containing coin bags, money carts (real bullion is heavy), and bullion boxes. Strangely, this "money" display in the midst of art is not as obtrusive as you might imagine.

THE CHINESE HISTORICAL SOCIETY OF AMERICA MUSEUM

A few feet west of the Pacific Heritage Museum, you will come to pocket-sized Grabhorn Park—a quiet place to eat a sandwich and get some air. A sign explains that the park is named after Edwin and Robert Grabhorn, who operated Grabhorn Press between 1933 and 1942.

Against a building at the end of this teensy park is an odd sculpture/fountain by Pepo Pichler. Above the fountain, you can see an ever-changing display of drying laundry hanging from windows, which creates a kind of "happening" out of the whole scene.

Fountain at the end of tiny Grabhorn Park

A few feet past the park is the doorway of the Chinese Historical Society of America Museum, which is in the basement of 650 Commercial. The interior—old, rickety, and even mildewed—is a total contrast to the other two museums you have seen. The Museum is open Tuesday through Friday from 10 A.M. to 4 P.M. and Saturday from 11 A.M. to 3 P.M.

You go down some narrow steps to get to the Museum, where you will see a fine display of old photos and text recounting the history of the Chinese people in America, including their impressive contributions to building the West. Don't expect any trendy, multimedia displays: there is no "eye candy" here. You have to read the text. I did and actually learned a lot. For example, I learned that in 1784, the Chinese imported ginseng root from *America*!

There are also some artifacts, including a Chinese Buddhist altar from 1880 and clothing and shoes worn by 19th century Chinese pioneers.

GETTING BACK

Piece of cake. Just continue on Commercial to Kearny. Turn left and walk back to the Banker's Heart.

Portsmouth Square

Portsmouth Square is definitely worth a look, not for what it is today—a glorified parking garage—but for what it once was—the place where San Francisco quickened. Even today, with the cheap bric-a-brac pagoda motif on the garage elevators and its meretricious gold elevator doors, this tiny park has more history packed into it than any area of comparable size in the city.

Today, it's hard to forgive the San Francisco administrators who, in 1960, built a parking garage under this incomparable piece of San Francisco history, a piece that once lost can never be reclaimed. (I guess, to them, "park" was a verb, not a noun.)

To understand Portsmouth Square, you must first realize that the original shoreline at the Square came up to what is now Montgomery Street. When you stood in the Square, Bay waters practically lapped at your ankles.

The Square was actually created by Swiss ship captain and engineer Jean Jacques Vioget, who was asked by *alcalde* (mayor and magistrate) Francisco de Haro to lay out Yerba Buena village—as San Francisco was then called—as a little town with real streets. In 1839, Vioget created a checkerboard of small blocks with a little plaza that faced the water. The plaza is today's Portsmouth Square. Vioget must have liked his work because he built his own house right across the plaza at Kearny and Clay.

In 1846 the United States and Mexico were at war over Texas, and on July 9, of that year, Captain John B. Montgomery and 70 soldiers and marines from the USS *Portsmouth* marched into the plaza and raised the America flag. Thus, Yerba Buena became part of the United States, and the plaza was named "Portsmouth Square."

Two years later, on May 12, 1848 the Portsmouth Square convulsed again as Sam Brannan, raced through it waving a vial of gold dust over

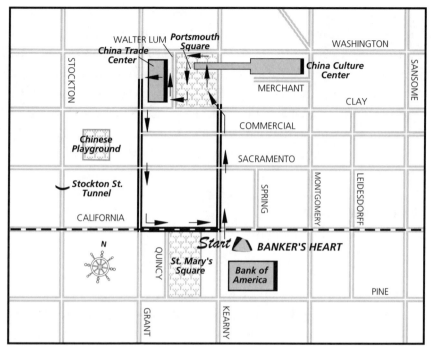

Portsmouth Square

his head and shouting "Gold! Gold! Gold on the American River." The stampede for gold was on. Brannan and 237 other Mormons had arrived in San Francisco in 1846 on the ship *Brooklyn*, hoping to meet Mormon leader Brigham Young and the main group of Mormons, who were actually in Salt Lake City. Talk about a bad sense of direction. Brannan soon became a local mover and shaker and started Yerba Buena's first newspaper, the *California Star*.

As though precipitating the Gold Rush wasn't enough, Brannan soon plunged the Square in further turmoil. At that time, gangs of "hoodlums" roamed the city. Most famous were the Sydney Ducks, largely made up of escapees from Australian penal colonies, and the Hounds, mostly ex-New Yorkers. The gangs owned the streets, robbing pedestrians, shanghaiing sailors, and demanding protection money from shop owners. Most nefarious were the six devastating fires set by the Sydney Ducks between December 24, 1849, and the spring of 1851.

Finally, Brannan had enough. He organized the Committee of Vigilance with himself as president. Its first victim was John Jenkins, a Sydney Duck, caught trying to steal a safe. The Committee hanged Jenkins in Portsmouth Square on June 10, 1851. That crimped the style of the Hounds and the Ducks, and the city stopped burning—for a while.

After the 1906 quake and fire, homeless San Franciscans camped in Portsmouth Square, as they did in Golden Gate Park, Mission Park, and, of course, the Presidio. Today, homeless San Franciscans still sleep in Portsmouth Square.

WALKING TIME

Up to 15 minutes round trip.

GETTING THERE

From the Banker's Heart at Kearny and California, walk north on Kearny to Clay. Cross Kearny, then Clay, and turn left. In a few feet, you will come to the entrance to the lower section of the Square. (To create the underground garage, the Square was sliced into lower and upper sections, with no way of getting from one section to the other except by leaving the Square entirely!)

THE SQUARE

Despite the "renovations," it's still enjoyable to sit in the Square and watch children play on the climbing structures and elderly Chinese men cluster 'round the bright red benches playing board games (I was too shy to march right up and see exactly *what* they were playing.) If you eat a sandwich in the Square, you may be sharing your bench with a sleeping homeless man.

The lower section contains benches, a large sandbox filled with climbing equipment for small children, and some ammonia-drenched concrete steps that lead from garage exits. It also contains a monument to Andrew Smith Hallidie, the English-born Scotsman, who "invented" cable cars. Hallidie, whose uncle was court physician to Queen Victoria, came to California and devised a steel cable system to work the gold and silver mines. In San Francisco, Hallidie supposedly was walking up a rainy San

Francisco hill in 1869 when he noticed an approaching car drawn by four horses. He watched as a horse slipped on the wet cobblestones and car and horses tumbled backward down the hill. No mention is made of the passengers' fate, but the poor horses broke many bones.

Moved by this sight, Hallidie built the first cable-car system, which took its test run down Clay Street—with Hallidie himself working both grip and brakes—on August 2, 1873. The monument at the Square reads: "Site of eastern terminus first street cars in world propelled by cable. Commenced operation 1873. Ceased February 15, 1942." The cable cars are still operating, so don't believe everything you read, even it's carved in stone.

Exit the lower tier of the Square at Washington and walk uphill to reenter the upper tier at the corner of Washington and Walter U. Lum Place. Here are more benches and play equipment, garage elevators, a functioning rest room, and four more monuments. Let's visit the monuments one-by-one:

Dedicated in 1897, a granite monument to Robert Louis Stevenson is topped by a model of the Hispañola, the ship in Stevenson's *Treasure Island*. Stevenson came to San Francisco in 1879, broke, unknown,

Playing board games at Portsmouth Square

consumptive, and lovesick. He was in pursuit of Fanny Van de Grift Osborne, who became his wife a year later, but who was still married to someone else at that time. Stevenson loved to sit on a bench in the Square, writing and presumable thinking about Fanny. On the monument is an excerpt from "A Christmas Sermon." The excerpt begins:

> *To be honest to be*
> *kind to earn a little*
> *to spend a little to*
> *make up on the whole a*
> *family happier for his*
> *presence...*

The next monument is at the site where John B. Montgomery, captain of the USS *Portsmouth* raised the first American flag in San Francisco on July 9, 1846.

Then, as you approach Clay Street, you will see a monument at the site of California's first public school, which opened April 3, 1848.

Most moving is the last monument, the 1994 Thomas Marsh's bronze sculpture of the *Goddess of Democracy*, which honors the statue of the same name that briefly stood in Tiananmen Square during the democracy

The Goddess of Democracy at Portsmouth Square

demonstrations in Beijing in 1989. Whenever I see Marsh's statue, I am reminded of Wang Weilin, the 19-year old factory worker's son, who stopped a column of tanks in Tiananmen Square in June of 1989 and who was later seen with his head shaven being paraded through the street with others destined for execution as criminals.

THE CHINESE CULTURE CENTER

When you're through enjoying the monuments and people, take the pedestrian walkway from the upper tier over Kearny Street to the China Culture Center. This is actually the third floor of the Chinatown Holiday Inn, which was once the site of the old Jenny Lind theater, and then later of a City Hall and jail. The walkway obscures the Holiday Inn pretty well and creates the illusion you are entering a quiet, private place.

Inside is a gallery that displays both Chinese contemporary and Chinese historical art. When I was last there, I saw a magnificent exhibit of Tibetan painted furniture and carpets. The gallery is open Tuesday through Sunday from 10 A.M. to 4 P.M. and is free.

The Center also sponsors community festivals, as well as classes in crafts, folk and ethnic dancing, cooking, and Chinese martial arts. And for tourists, there is a Chinese Heritage Walk. This is not free.

GETTING BACK

If you are in a hurry, just exit the Square and walk back down Kearny to the Banker's Heart.

If you have a few extra minutes, exit the Square at the corner of Washington and Walter U. Lum Place, and then enter the overbearing Empress of China/China Trade Center building in the middle of the block. You will actually be entering through a shop called Chong Imports (35 Walter U. Lum Place), which sells everything from dried ducks—flat as pancakes—to acupuncture needles. Walk toward the back of the shop, then up the steps, and exit. You will be on Grant Avenue. Turn left to walk down Grant toward California, enjoying the shops—some traditional, some schlock. At California, turn left again to return to the Banker's Heart.

WALK 13 City Lights

In 1968, a few years after I came to San Francisco, I mailed Lawrence Ferlinghetti all my poems so he could publish them in a book. He declined, but he did write me a nice note, which I am reprinting here. (A few years later, my poems were published by shameless hussy—a great women's press. Eat your heart out Lawrence.)

Lawrence Ferlinghetti opened City Lights Bookstore in 1953, hoping that the profits would support his journal, also called *City Lights*. (The name comes from the Charlie Chaplin movie.) The journal folded but the bookstore thrived. City Lights soon become a home for the San

CITY LIGHTS BOOKS
261 COLUMBUS AVENUE, SAN FRANCISCO 11

6/11/68

Dear Gail — There are many wonderful lines in these poems — especially "Sweeping his agony across the heath"

All in all, not enough for a book, I feel. Try a few on places like "Evergreen Review" (Grove Press) and tell them I sent you.....

Sorry to be so long — Lawrence (Ferlinghetti)

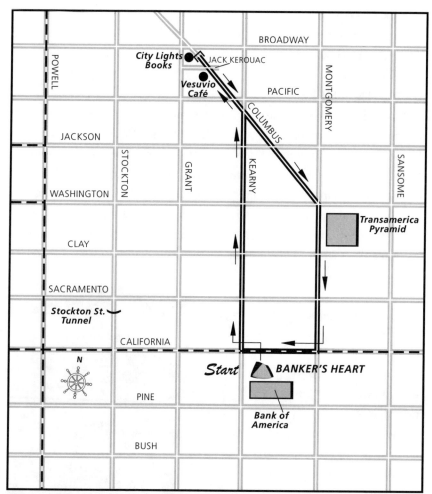

City Lights

Francisco beat writers of the '50s—Alan Ginsberg, Jack Kerouac, Gary Snyder, Gregory Corso, Philip Whalen, and others.

Today City Lights is operated as a collective, but I've been told that sometimes you can see Ferlinghetti working around the store. City Lights publishing company, which published Alan Ginsberg's *Howl*, is also still operating.

WALKING TIME

Twenty minutes round trip. Remember: this is *not* counting the time you spend browsing in the bookstore.

GETTING THERE

From the Banker's Heart at Kearny and California, walk north on Kearny Street. Just past Jackson, turn left (northwest) on Columbus. Walk up Columbus on the left side of the street until you come to Vesuvio's on the corner of Columbus and Jack Kerouac Alley. This is an old-time beat hangout and a great place to have a beer and contemplate life. A sign painted above the window says "We are Itching to Get Away from Portland Oregon." I'm not sure what this means, but for sure it's significant. Dylan Thomas used to drink here. Also Lawrence Ferlinghetti and Alan Ginsberg.

Cross Jack Kerouac Alley and you are at the City Lights Bookstore.

Note: right before you get to Columbus, you'll come to the House of Nanking (919 Kearny). This incredibly wonderful and inexpensive eatery is so crowded that if you want to eat lunch here, plan on coming at 11 a.m. to get a seat.

CITY LIGHTS

City Lights is not a bookstore that has everything. Rather, it's a bookstore where you'll feel that every book has been lovingly selected with you in mind.

City Lights building at the corner of Jack Kerouac Alley and Columbus

Inside, it's worn and a little dark, but luxuriant with old-time ambiance. It even smells warm, woody, and friendly. You almost expect a beat poet to stroll past at any moment—and often one does. To the right as you walk in is a wonderful collection of new fiction, non-fiction, published journals, and just plain "literature," *i.e.*, famous books by famous authors. A plaque lets you know that you are in a national landmark— the first paper-back bookstore in the nation (maybe in the world).

If you venture further to the right, you come to a narrow flight of stairs. At the top is a room full of beat literature, poetry, books published by City Lights, and used books.

Back by the entrance, you can go down a flight of old wooden steps to the lowest floor. Community announcements line the staircase walls. When I used to browse at City Lights in the late '60s, the bottom floor was stuffed with small-press stapled-backed books that probably never sold two copies. It's a little more commercially viable now, but the book sections still have names like "Anarchism" and "Class War." There's even a little table downstairs and a few chairs, as though the owners know you're planning to read the books without buying them, and that's OK too.

GETTING BACK WITH DETOUR THROUGH THE TRANSAMERICA PYRAMID

If you have any money left when you leave City Lights (it's really hard to leave this store without buying a book), stop at Vesuvio's for a quick drink before heading back to work. Somehow, I feel this isn't the right place to ask for Calistoga water.

To vary the route back, continue down Columbus past Kearny to Montgomery for a look at the Transamerica Pyramid (600 Montgomery), which at 853 feet beats out the Bank of America World Headquarters for the distinction of being the tallest building in San Francisco. The Pyramid's size and shape caused enormous controversy when the building was constructed in the early '70s, but San Franciscan's have mostly come to accept it, and some even like it.

Alas, when I tried to take the elevator to the Pyramid's observatory on the 27th floor, the guard told me that observatory was permanently inaccessible to visitors "for security reasons," but you can still enjoy the paintings in the lobby as well as the pretty fountain in Redwood Park on the east side of the building. During the summer months, there's music in the park on Fridays at lunchtime.

A plaque in the lobby informs you that this is the site of the Montgomery Block, a four-story 1853 luxury building that once housed the best of San Francisco's business community. Stockbrokers, realtors, doctors, and lawyers had offices here, as did San Francisco's first law library, the U.S. Army Corps of Engineers, and two newspapers—the *Alta California* and the *Daily Herald*. The building later evolved into a low-rent rooming house for artists, writers, and musicians. Bret Harte, Ambrose Bierce, Jack London, and Joaquin Miller apparently hung out in the bar and steam baths. Dr. Sun Yat-sen wrote the proclamation of the Republic of China from his second-floor office. In 1959, the "Monkey Block," as it was now called, was torn down and made into a parking lot.

After leaving the Transamerica Pyramid, continue down Montgomery. At California, turn right to the Banker's Heart.

Crocker Galleria & Maiden Lane

If you were born with a defective shopping gene as I was, and you don't like shopping, you have to work a little to make shopping tours exciting. But it definitely can be done.

WALKING TIME

About 25 minutes, not counting time spent exploring shops in the Crocker Galleria, but counting time spent walking up and down Maiden Lane.

GETTING THERE

From the Banker's Heart at Kearny and California, walk south on Kearny until you cross Sutter. Then turn left and go to the entrance to the Crocker Galleria about halfway down the block.

But before you enter, you *must* turn around and look up at the Hallidie Building (130–150 Sutter) directly across the street. I must confess that before I learned about this building, I thought of it simply as the "post office," since this is where I mailed letters on my way to work. However, after reading about the Hallidie Building, I looked up one day and realized how exquisite the structure is.

Designed by San Francisco architect Willis Polk in 1917, the Hallidie Building is the world's first "glass-curtain walled" building. So what's a glass-curtain walled building? Well, the glass and metal facade is not part of the building's support structure, but hangs in front of it like an elegant curtain. Notice the delicate fire escapes that look as if they were crocheted from spun metal strands by my grandmother.

CROCKER GALLERIA

Walk down the steps into the Crocker Galleria. This three-story, sky-light-domed pavilion is modeled after Milan's Galleria Vittorio

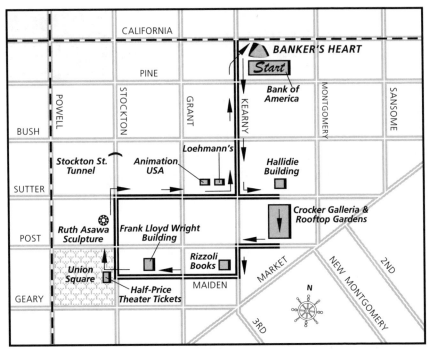

Crocker Galleria and Maiden Lane

Emmanuelle and continues the glass theme of the Hallidie Building, only in a very different way. Designed in 1982 by Skidmore, Owings & Merrill, the Galleria consists of a complex of luxury fashion shops, restaurants, and specialty boutiques. Set under the glass dome are also café tables, topiaries of English ivy, and pots of geraniums and impatiens.

On the first level, set incongruously amidst boutiques with names like Mizani, Adornme, and Versace, is the Hospitality House Shop & Gallery, which sells artwork by homeless and low-income artists from San Francisco's Tenderloin. Actually, I lived in the Tenderloin when I first came to San Francisco from New York in 1965, so I have a soft spot in my heart for this troubled neighborhood. I had found an apartment at Hyde and Eddy Streets, and, unlike my former Manhattan apartment, this one had hardwood floors and no cockroaches, so for an all too brief time I mistakenly thought I was in paradise.

At the shop, you can see paintings, pottery, sculpture, drawings, and greeting cards. Last time I was there, a genuine Tenderloin artist was on site, ensconced in front of his easel, painting away. Hospitality House also hosts solo shows by its artists.

After exploring the shops on the first two levels, take the elevator to the top floor. Here are restaurants, decent restrooms, and the entrance to *two* rooftop gardens. On the west side, near the Faz restaurant, are steps up to the smaller garden, called the Rooftop Terrace. This little-used outdoor space offers comfortable wood-slat benches, potted plants, and a good view of the Hallidie Building. It also offers privacy since hardly anyone comes here—maybe because the odor of cooking food can be very strong. A mini-running track (1/16th of a mile) circles the garden's perimeter.

Steps to the more popular garden, called the Roof Garden, are on the east side, near the Chili Up restaurant. You can actually see this garden from Montgomery and Market if you look up at the rooftop of One Montgomery. Crocker Bank agreed to provide this open space as part of a deal allowing it to build the Galleria and the adjacent Pacific Telesis building. In addition, Crocker Bank agreed to preserve the historic

Crocker Galleria

The glass-domed Crocker Galleria

Banking Hall of One Montgomery, also designed by Willis Polk. In fact, you can actually take the elevator from One Montgomery (now owned by Wells Fargo) up to this garden.

This open space is a little more lush and a lot more popular than the other, judging from the number of people I saw relaxing on the benches and eating brown-bag lunches. When I was there, marigolds and bougainvillea were blooming. At other times, you can see azaleas and jasmine in bloom. There is also a small fountain and a big brass sundial. Best of all, you can stare down on busy Market Street from above and feel enjoyably removed from the bustle.

MAIDEN LANE

Exit the Crocker Galleria on Post Street. Before you proceed, however, look across the street at the Mechanics' Institute Library (57 Post). This is an excellent library (membership is $60 a year) and a superb resource for book-lovers who work downtown. Chugging along since 1854, today the Mechanic's Institute Library provides books, magazines, and videos to the financial-district crowd. Best of all, inside it looks like an old-time library, it smells like a library, and it's stuffed with books and helpful librarians. You can reserve and check out materials, do research, and make requests for purchases. Free tours are offered every Wednesday at noon. Check it out.

Now, on with the walk. Turn right to cross Kearny. Then turn left on Kearny to the brass-gated entrance to Maiden Lane, a two-block alley closed to street traffic and home to trendy shops, outdoor cafés, and also to San Francisco's only building designed by Frank Lloyd Wright.

Maiden Lane was once Maiden "Not" Lane. Known as Morton Street, in the late 19th century this alley was infamous for its brothels. These establishments weren't even real houses but instead tiny makeshift structures known as "cribs" from which women, naked from the waist up, would lean from windows, offering their services.

Morton Street burned in the 1906 fire and was rebuilt as a quieter, chaster place. It was first renamed Union Square Avenue, then Manila Avenue, but neither name took hold. Then, in 1922, Alfred Samuels, a jeweler, picked the name Maiden Lane. And Maiden Lane it is.

As you enter, you will see the Iron Horse Restaurant on your left, which according to the *Bay Guardian*, has a great happy hour with free hors d'oeuvres. On your right, a little further along, is the back entrance to Rizzoli Books, a wonderfully browsable book store with convenient noon-hour readings by top-selling authors. I heard John Berendt, author of *Midnight in the Garden of Good and Evil*, read here.

Be careful crossing at Grant as there is no traffic light or crosswalk. You can often hear music in this part of the alley—local performers serenading diners at their outdoor tables, which are right in the street. Last time I was there, a bass player and a trumpet player were belting out "As Time Goes By."

The Frank Lloyd Wright building on Maiden Lane

At 140 Maiden Lane is the alley's crown jewel, San Francisco's only building designed by Frank Lloyd Wright. Built in 1949 as the V.C. Morris Gift shop and later home to the Circle Gallery, this beautiful structure offers circles on the outside of its brick exterior and circles on the inside. Under circular lights, a spiral ramp takes you from one floor to the next. (In fact, this building is often considered a precursor of the Guggenheim in New York, which expands on the swirl design.) The rooms, the fixtures, the lights, the huge hanging plant—they're all circles. The place is circle city.

In late December of 1997, Folk Art International, Xanadu Tribal Arts Gallery, and Boretti Amber & Design moved into the building. The new owner, Raymond Handley has worked to restore the structure to its original appearance, even reintroducing some of the Wright's original furniture. The building is a little masterpiece. Don't miss it!

Maiden Lane ends at Stockton, smack at the discount ticket kiosk, which offers half-price tickets for current-day theater performances.

GETTING BACK

If you wish, you can return the same way you came, crossing to the opposite side of Maiden Lane to explore shops you missed the first time around.

Or, for variety, you can exit on Stockton. If you do, cross Stockton and head north to view the Ruth Asawa sculpture and fountain at the entrance of the Grand Hyatt Hotel at 345 Stockton. Notice the incredibly intricate figures—creatures and golems of all types—pressed into the dark base of the fountain.

Then turn right on Sutter back to Kearny. At 222 Sutter, you will pass Animation USA, a not-at-all-stuffy gallery of animation art where you are welcome to come in and look at pictures of your favorite cartoon characters. At the same address is also the fashion-discount store Loehmann's, the direct descendant of the Loehmann's on Fordham Road in the Bronx where, in the Fifties, as a broke teenager, I spent many Saturday afternoons trying to piece together outfits that I could afford with my minuscule resources.

At Kearny, turn left to return to the Banker's Heart.

Stacey's & Alexander Book Company WALK 15

My friend Judith says, "Always buy books at independently owned bookstores." Stacey's and Alexander Book Company are both independently owned, but Stacey's is awfully big—actually a chain of three stores— so whenever I buy a book there, to appease my guilt I instantly run across to Alexander Book Company and buy a book there too.

WALKING TIME

About 25 minutes. (Lots of traffic lights slow you down!)

GETTING THERE

From the Banker's Heart at Kearny and California, walk east on California to Montgomery, turn right and continue to Market. At noon, the streets will be jammed with financial-district workers.

Turn left at Market and cross Market on the east side of Second Street. You will be at the Rand McNally map store (595 Market). Take a few minutes to browse in the window of this wonderful shop or, better yet, go in. This store special-ordered maps of Ukraine for me when I was transcribing an oral history of my dad. When the maps came, they were in Cyrillic, but who said it's a perfect world?

Continue east to Stacey's at 581 Market.

STACEY'S

Stacey's is a bookstore that seems to have everything. Its professional section— computing, business, engineering, medicine, and science—is the largest I've ever seen, and I, personally, have dropped a nice chunk of change on the computer-books counter. Stacey's medical book selection is gigantic, and, if you're so inclined, you can just stand around and look up rare diseases you imagine you have. No one will bother you.

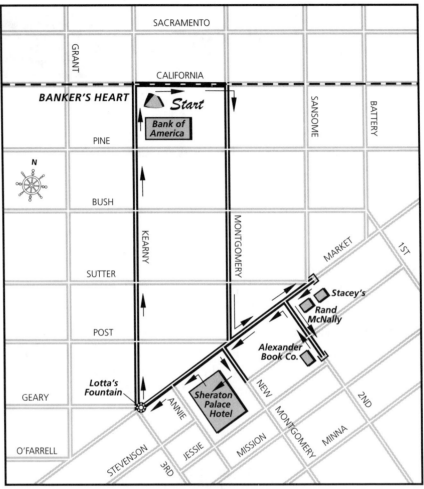

Stacey's and Alexander Book Company

Opened in 1923 by John W. Stacey and a group of California doctors, Stacey's currently has stores in San Francisco, Palo Alto. and Cupertino. The San Francisco store recently expanded to add 7,500 more feet of space for books.

Of course, now I can't find anything, and this makes me terribly crotchety. The computer books that used to be crowded together in the basement are now floating somewhere in the top-floor stratosphere. But I know that eventually I'll get used to the changes and start buying books again.

Stacey's has author readings at lunchtime and also after work. Pick up a schedule at the counter. They will cheerfully special-order books for you.

THE ALEXANDER BOOK COMPANY

What self-confidence to open next to Stacey's!

To get to the Alexander Book Company, turn left when you leave Stacey's, cross Second, turn left again, and continue to a friendly little gray building with an old-fashioned fire escape winding down the front. This is the Alexander Book Company at 50 Second Street.

This jewel of a bookstore is as intimate as Stacey's is expansive. Inside, the bright blue banisters and light wood shelves give you the feeling of browsing in a homey family library. Despite its small-shop feel, however, this bookstore is amazingly well-stocked and actually comprises three floors.

Opened in 1990 by Bonnie and Michael Stuppin (sister and brother), Alexander Book Company got its start in an interesting way. Michael was working for B. Dalton in New York, but quit in protest when Dalton yanked Salman Rushdie's *The Satanic Verses* off the shelf. He then came

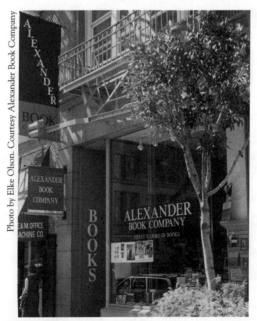

The Alexander Book Company

to San Francisco and opened the Alexander Book Company with Bonnie.

Alexander Book Company's claim to fame is its Sister Circle, a literary forum focused on women of color, but open to everyone. Guests have included luminaries such as Alice Walker, Nikki Giovanni, Anna Deavere Smith, and Ntozake Shange. Sister Circle meets at 12:30 on various weekdays. One Friday a month at 12:30, the Sister Circle *Forum*, a "rap session" offshoot of the Sister Circle, gathers to discuss topics of special interest. Some recent topics: Women of Color Bodybuilders, Black Women in Corporate America, Black Women in the Media, and The Hair Thing. You can pick up schedules at the front of the store.

Alexander Book Company also publishes a bimonthly newsletter, *Alexander's Book Column*, which pays $50 for reader's book reviews. They didn't publish mine, but you might have better luck.

The store has lots of events, readings, and signings, and will order anything for you that's in print.

GETTING BACK WITH DETOUR THROUGH THE PALACE HOTEL

To return, walk back to Market and turn left. When you get to New Montgomery, cross and turn left again. Then, cut through the Palace Hotel (2 New Montgomery) for a quick look at the Garden Court.

Built by silver baron Billy Ralston in 1875, the Palace Hotel (today the Sheraton Palace), was once the largest hotel in America. Considered a bit much even in its heyday, the Palace once boasted gold dinner service, imported linens, and an atrium capacious enough to accommodate horses and carriages. Despite the Hotel's modern (for then) fire-detection system, it burnt to the ground in the 1906 post-quake fire.

Rebuilt in 1909, the Palace Hotel today offers the magnificent Garden Court, which you will see as soon as you enter. The huge vaulted ceiling, the marble columns, and the glittering chandeliers create a sensation of elegance not to be missed. You can have afternoon tea there for $18.

Turn right at the Garden Court, walk through the hotel, and exit on Market.

Continue west. At Third Street, cross Market. In a traffic island at Market and Kearny, notice Lotta's Fountain. Considered lovably ugly, this fountain was given to the city in 1875 by Lotta Crabtree, a popular singer, actress, and music-hall performer. At one time, the fountain had cups chained to it so people could drink, although this wouldn't seem very sanitary today. In the days following the '06 quake and fire, survivors gathered here to reconnect with family and friends. Since then, quake survivors and others have gathered at Lotta's Fountain at 5:13 a.m. every April 18, for a remembrance. These days, it is pretty much others.

Continue north on Kearny to return to the Banker's Heart.

WALK 16 Aerobic Walk to Grace Cathedral

For a brisk, aerobic walk that gets your heart rate singing, walk straight up California Street to Grace Cathedral at the top of Nob Hill.[6] This walk will give you a chance to mingle with San Francisco's hoity toity and also to view the city at its elegant best. The Hill is sometimes known as "snob hill," and the walk is a good way to take a rest from San Francisco's urban problems.

No matter how dreary, shadowed, and fog-filled downtown San Francisco, the sun always seems to shine on Nob Hill. I'm not sure whether this is because the Hill pokes above the fog or because the shadows of the Nob Hill buildings fall on the downtown streets below, while nothing shadows Nob Hill. Whatever the reason, the top of the Hill always seems glorious. You feel you're on top of the world.

WALKING TIME

Banker's Heart to Grace Cathedral and back, including the side trip down the Joice Alley steps and the Ritz-Carlton detour, took me 30 minutes.

GETTING THERE

Getting there couldn't be easier. From the Banker's Heart, cross California and walk straight uphill (west) on California. The cable car will be jingling along beside you. Where you break a sweat depends upon your aerobic conditioning, but you'll definitely break one before you get to the top. Me, I'm usually sweating by Grant Avenue (one block away).

---

[6] The *San Francisco Woman's Travel Guide* by Harriet Swift (Berkeley: Book Passage Press, 1994), p.88, suggests that the name comes from either "Knob" Hill because the hill is one big knob or from "Nabob" Hill because of all the nabobs that lived there.

Make sure to look in the window of the Twin's Armoire Boutique at 860 California, between Stockton and Powell. It's filled with fascinating objects that defy categorization. Most are a little too big for what my mother would have described as *chotchkes*.

When you get to Mason Street, you'll see the luxurious Mark Hopkins Hotel on the left side of California and the equally luxurious Fairmont Hotel on the right. If you're ready for a break from your aerobic activities, walk into the Fairmont and ride the exterior glass elevator from the ground floor to the 22nd floor of the Fairmont tower.

You don't have to pretend you're a guest to do this. They *like* you and *want* you to come in. Just walk in the front entrance, continue straight

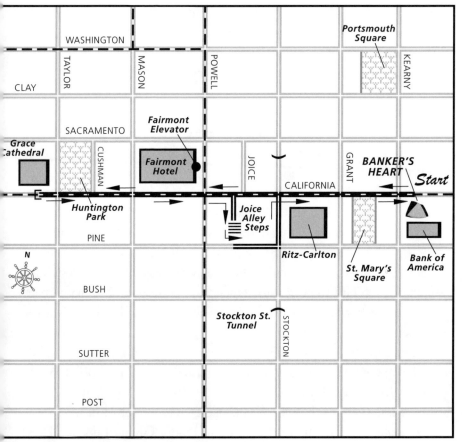

Aerobic Walk to Grace Cathedral

back, turn left when you come to the double doors, and follow the signs. It's free and the views of the city are unequaled. (Warning: If you fear heights, this ride is a challenge.)

Across Mason on the right side of the street is the dark brownstone Pacific Union Club. Here, they don't like you and don't want you to come in, as the Pacific Union Club is one of the most exclusive men's clubs in the country. Built in 1886 by James Flood as his personal mansion, the structure was rebuilt as the Pacific Union Club in 1912 by architect Willis Polk. It looks like a gentlemen's club straight out of an Edith Wharton novel. In recent years, the Club has faced a number of lawsuits because of it's "all male" character.

Past the Pacific Union Club, you'll come to pretty Huntington Park, where you can take another rest if you need one. This tiny urban jewel is maintained by private as well as city funds. It offers benches, fountains, sculptures, a sandbox, and a playground.

Cross Taylor Street, and you're at Grace Cathedral.

GRACE CATHEDRAL

The site of this majestic Episcopalian church has a not-so-religious history. The story goes that railroad baron Charles Crocker wished to buy a tiny cottage from undertaker Nicholas Yung to complete his holdings on the block where Grace Cathedral now stands. When Yung, a German immigrant, refused to sell at Crocker's offered price, Crocker built a 40-foot high "spite fence" around Yung's cottage, plunging it into darkness. In 1877, Denis Kearney, a San Francisco political organizer, who hated both immigrants and the railroad barons who brought them West, led a mob up Nob Hill to protest the fence. The protesters were beaten back by police. After Yung's death, Crocker's heirs were finally able to buy the property.

Grace Cathedral was built over many years. The cornerstone was laid in 1910, but the actual consecration did not take place until 1964. In 1993, the old parish hall on Taylor Street was demolished, allowing the Cathedral to appear in full view like a crown atop Nob Hill.

Outside the church are the beautiful bronze Ghiberti doors. (These are copies of Lorenzo Ghiberti's doors to the Baptistery in Florence known as the *Doors of Paradise*. The originals were hidden from Nazis during World War II.)

Inside, on the left, is a statue of Saint Francis by San Francisco's beloved Beniamino Bufano. The stained glass windows in the nave depict spiritual leaders from Moses to Martin Luther King. Wall murals by Antonio Sotomayer, tracing the cathedral's history, are inside the chapel as are exquisite needle-point kneelers painstakingly made by women church members.

Best of all for a walker is the "labyrinth" inside the front entrance. This 35-foot wide maze, painted on canvas, is a replica of the design in the stone floor of the Chartres Cathedral in France. Walking the maze is considered a mystical experience— "a palpable mix of solemnity and joy." Take off your shoes.

Literature published by the Cathedral says "There are three stages of the walk: the first (until you reach the center of the Labyrinth) is purgatory—a releasing, a letting go of the details of your life....The second— Illumination— is when you reach the center....As you leave, following the same path out of the center as you came in upon, you enter the third

Photo by Steven Jenner

The outdoor labyrinth

stage—Union—which is joining God, your Higher Power or the healing forces at work in the world."

In September of 1995, an outdoor version of the labyrinth opened in the plaza to the right of the main entrance as a memorial to Jewish philanthropist and church benefactor Mel Swig. You can keep your shoes on as you walk the outdoor version.

GETTING BACK

On your return to work, detour down the beautiful stairway in Joice Alley. To get there, walk down California on the south side of the street. When you pass Powell, start looking for Joice Alley. (If you get to Stockton, you've come too far). Turn right into Joice and walk toward Pine Street. Before you get to Pine, you will come to a gracious, wide, concrete stairway that opens into Pine Street.[7] Descend. On the right, near the landing, is a small shrine to St. Francis. Once when I was there, a healthy looking impatiens plant was growing out of a sidewalk crack.

Walk downhill on Pine and cross Stockton. Then look up at the magnificent and luxurious Ritz-Carlton Hotel that takes up the entire block of Stockton between Pine and California. On Stockton walk back up to California so you can get a complete view of one of the world's ritziest hotels.

On California walk downhill to return to the Banker's Heart.

---

[7] For making me aware of this stairway, I am grateful to Adah Bakalinsky and her book *Stairway Walks of San Francisco* (Berkeley, Wilderness Press), 1995

The Cable Car Barn/Museum WALK 17

The thing I like best about this museum is that it's not a museum. It's real. It's the actual powerhouse that powers the cables. Inside, you see the moving cables which—at that moment—are holding the cable cars onto the hills of San Francisco. You realize, anew, that the tourist-filled cable cars careening down those hills are in fact just big wooden boxes with no engine or motor. (They do have brakes though.)

WALKING TIME

Allow a shade under half an hour for this walk. If you take the Ross Alley detour, add another five or ten minutes.

GETTING THERE

From the Banker's Heart at Kearny and California, cross Kearny and head north. Just past Sacramento, you will come to Commercial Street (known as "Brothel Row" after the '06 quake). Glance to your left to see splotches of the original red brick once used for paving most San Francisco streets.

Continue walking to Washington. Then turn left up the gentle hill.

At once, you are in the crowded, narrow streets of Chinatown. enveloped by restaurants, markets, souvenir shops, and trading companies with their windows filled with dried sea slugs, birds' nests, sea horses, and shark fins.

Just past Grant you will come to the infamous Sam Wo's (813 Washington), known among the Fifties' beats and Sixties' hippies as "the cheapest Chinese restaurant in town." It is somewhat less well known as the place where my husband, Pete, proposed to me (with suitable encouragement) 29 years ago. When I went back recently, I discovered that the restaurant had barely changed one iota in almost three decades.

Sam Wo's on Washington Street

You still walk through the incredibly narrow kitchen to get to the equally narrow seating area on the second and third floors. You still wobble on the same rickety stools. The food still arrives from the kitchen via an ancient dumbwaiter. It's true our old waiter, Edsel Ford Fong, famous as the world's rudest waiter, wasn't there to scream at us and make us write our order down on paper scraps.[8] But, the food (I'm talking noodles) is still the cheapest in town.

Sam Wo's is open until 3 A.M. for those who like to eat lunch late. Or very early.

---

[8] In an article "The Fall of the House of Edsel" in the May 2, 1993, Image section of the Sunday *San Francisco Chronicle*, writer Gary Kamiya remembers Edsel Ford Fong, "No sooner would a group sit down than he would throw down a load of silverware and cups and instruct them to 'Set table.' If the mood struck him, he would force them to set other tables as well. I once ate an entire meal while he screamed at a hapless woman to 'Clear tables, Dolores! Dolores, serve tea!'"

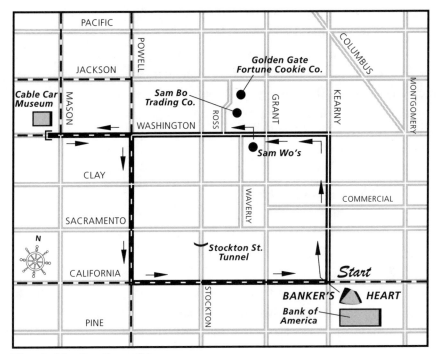

The Cable Car Barn/Museum

If you survive Sam Wo's, look for Waverly Place, which stretches south from Washington to Sacramento streets. Glance down this street to see the pretty balconies painted in bright red and green. As an ex-New Yorker, I recognized that the balconies are actually fire escapes, but fire escapes taken to the level of art.

Much more interesting to me is mysterious Ross Alley, stretching north between Washington and Jackson. (Please be careful if you cross Washington in the middle of the block.) If you have time, definitely wander down this narrow lane to feel transported out of time and place.

Exotic music from the hair-cutting salon fills the alley. The window of the Sam Bo Trading Company (14 Ross Alley) offers goods—Buddhas, lanterns, shrines—that I guarantee you will not have seen before. As you walk along you will pass a flower shop, jewelry stores, a printing shop, tiny garment "factories," and toward the end, the Golden Gate Fortune Cookie Company (56 Ross Alley), where, if you can crowd in, you can actually watch fortune cookies being churned out by the experienced two-person assembly team.

Continue down Washington. After Stockton, the congestion eases. To your left is the Commodore-Stockton elementary school. At lunch, small children play in the schoolyard so peacefully and sweetly, it's hard to imagine that urban problems exist.

At the corner of Washington and Mason, you will come to the Museum (1201 Mason).

THE CABLE CAR MUSEUM

The Museum is open 10 A.M. to 6 P.M. daily, and it's free. Before you enter, walk up Mason and peek into the barn. This is where the cable cars sleep at night and also where they get maintained.

Introduced to San Francisco in 1873 by Andrew Hallidie, the cable car system once contained more than 600 cars and 100 miles of track. Today, there are only three lines (Powell-Mason, Powell-Hyde, and California) and a mere 12 miles of track. But the cars still work the same way.

The cable car moves forward when the gripman squeezes a lever (a grip) that grasps the moving cable through a cut in the pavement. To brake, the gripman releases the cable, and the brakeman starts braking. The two communicate via the ringing bells. So, when you ride the cable cars, you are hanging off steep hills with absolutely nothing holding you on except the gripman's grip.

When you enter the museum, first walk downstairs to see the Sheave room. Through a glass wall, you look underneath Mason at Washington at the "guts" of the system—the actual underground sheaves and pulleys that spin the giant loops of cable into tunnels under San Francisco's streets. There are four cable loops, one for each street that sports a cable car: Powell, Mason, Hyde, and California.

Walk back upstairs, and from the viewing area, look down at the winding machinery—the motors, gears, and wheels that power the system. (Yes, there is a motor somewhere.) Most impressive are the gigantic spinning wheels—the driving and idler sheaves that regulate the cable movement and the tension sheave that keeps the cable taut.

The museum also displays lots of cable-car memorabilia—old tokens and transfers, as well as the famous Car No. 8, the only surviving cable car from Hallidie's original fleet, which ran on Clay Street from the top of Nob Hill to down to Portsmouth Square.

There is also a gift shop where you a purchase post cards, T-shirts, souvenirs, and lots of books about cable cars.

GETTING BACK

Since this is a "cable-car" walk, it's time to see some cable cars. Walk back along Washington one block to Powell street. Then start walking uphill (south) on Powell following the cable car line. At each corner, look to your left to enjoy sweeping views of the Bay.

Keep walking until you come to California Street. Then, turn left and follow the California cable car line down Nob Hill (east), back to the Banker's Heart.

As you walk up Powell and down California, it's cable cars all the way. You will see and hear them rolling past. You will feel like part of a magnificent picture postcard of quintessential San Francisco. After your museum excursion, though, you may feel differently about the tourists you see hanging off the cars with trusting, expectant faces.

You may say a prayer for them.

A Gallery Sampler

It's an arty town. There are two big gallery clusters in San Francisco—one south of Market near Yerba Buena Gardens and the other north of Market near Union Square. This walk covers the Union Square batch. Although there are probably forty or more galleries here, they're clumped together in only a few buildings, so they're easy to find.

This tour does *not* intend to be a definitive list of downtown galleries or of the "best" ones. I simply picked some that caught my fancy as I wandered around. Take the walk, and then explore some of the other galleries on your own. Trust your judgment. "I know what I like" is a valid yardstick when it comes to art.

Gallery days and hours vary, but most are closed on Tuesdays. For exact times, pick up the free San Francisco Bay Area Gallery Guide at 1369 Fulton Street (phone 415 921-1600). Or better yet, visit a gallery to pick one up. Galleries that are members of the San Francisco Art Dealers Association stay open the first Thursday evening of the month to accommodate those misguided connoisseurs who eat lunch at their desks.

WALKING TIME

The actual walking time is only 20 minutes. However, to this you must add the time you plan to spend inside the galleries.

GETTING THERE

From the Banker's Heart at Kearny and California, walk south on Kearny to Sutter. Turn right and enter the large modern building at 250 Sutter.

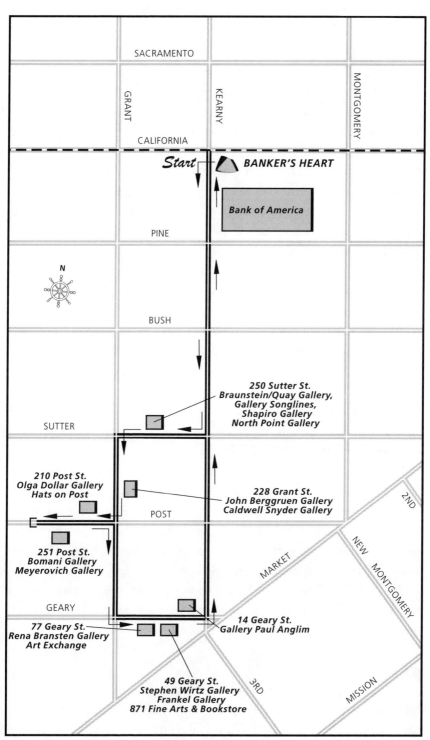

A Gallery Sampler

SUTTER STREET

Take the sleek, silvery elevator up to the third floor and enter the Braunstein/Quay Gallery. This large, light, open space displays contemporary fine art—painting, sculpture, and drawing—and also some performance art. The gallery has a wonderfully painty smell and moveable walls that create custom-made spaces for each exhibition. On display during my visit was "The Great Hunting and Fishing Expo!" by The Art Guys (Texans Jack Massing & Michael Galbreath). This outrageous mixture of taxidermy and sculpture, was either funny, sad, or infuriating, depending upon how you viewed the much-altered beasts on display.

To enter a different world, enter Gallery Songlines, which shows Aboriginal art of Australia. When I was there, I was captivated by the acrylic-on-canvas abstract paintings that curator David Betz explained to me were an extension of an ancient, and less permanent, method of producing art. The paintings I saw did not fit into any set categories—primitive, tribal, or modern abstract—but were enthralling.

Down the hall is the Shapiro Gallery, which features black and white, 20th century, classic photography. Depending upon the show, you can look at pictures of poor New Yorkers in the '40s or expansive Ansel Adams scenes of Yosemite. There are also wonderful books of photographs that you're welcome to browse through.

Now, to enter a still different world, take the elevator up to the fourth floor to the North Point Gallery, which displays realistic scenes by California 19th to early 20th century painters. (The gallery was on North Point for 25 years; hence the name.) This gallery also displays representational paintings by several California contemporary artists. The keyword is "representational." There's no abstract art here.

This gallery is like an old fashioned living room with comfy couches where you can sit and rest. While you're resting, you're also welcome to browse through the gallery's comprehensive library of California art books.

GRANT AVENUE

After you leave 250 Sutter, walk right to Grant, then turn left to the John Berggruen Gallery at 228 Grant. This gallery, which occupies three floors, displays 20th century American and European painting, sculpture, drawings, and prints. The John Berggruen Gallery is considered "top of the line," and a place where serious art connoisseurs shop. In the gallery's 25th anniversary catalog, curator John Berggruen describes himself as "still the mild-mannered, modest shopkeeper that you have all grown to tolerate."

In the early years, the gallery specialized in prints. But today the gallery also shows drawings and paintings by East Coast artists, classical European printmakers, and West Coast contemporary artists.

On the upper two floors of the same building is the Caldwell Synder Gallery, which features American and European contemporary artists. This gallery has represented the work of many women artists.

POST STREET

After exiting from 228 Grant, continue south to Post and turn right. At 210 Post is the Olga Dollar Gallery, which shows contemporary American painting, drawing, and sculpture. The gallery tends to display the work of young, energetic artists, rather than the work of more established figures.

You can look out the window of Olga Dollar right into the window of John Berggruen. That's sort of an art "happening" right there.

On the same floor as Olga Dollar, is Hats on Post, a millinery shop extraordinaire. Make sure to peek into this teensy salon, jumbled floor to ceiling with hats of every ilk—pillboxes, cloches, and turbans. There are even hats with moving parts—performance art, without a doubt! In this shop, you can get hats individually made, trimmed, and blocked.

Cross Post and enter 251 Post, a building with many galleries. One favorite is the Bomani Gallery on the sixth floor, owned by Asake Bomani and her husband, actor Danny Glover. This gallery emphasizes works by African-American artists.

Also in this building is the Meyerovich Gallery on the fourth floor, which is like a little museum, with paintings, lithographs, and etchings by Lichtenstein, Matisse, Chagall, Picasso, Motherwell, and Miró. The sliding walls and adjustable lights display the works to great advantage, and the proud and helpful owner, Alexander Meyerovich, will gladly show you around.

GEARY STREET

After you leave Post Street, return to Grant and walk south one block to Geary. At 77 Geary, you will find another cluster of galleries. Two of my favorites, both on the second floor, are the Rena Bransten Gallery and the Art Exchange.

The Rena Bransten Gallery shows ceramics, painting, sculpture, and installations by contemporary artists from all over the United States and Europe.[9] There is also emphasis on photography, video, and conceptual art by both established and emerging artists.

Right outside the door of the Rena Bransten Gallery is the Art Exchange, which sells "pre-owned" contemporary art. Owning a pre-owned painting is better than owning a pre-owned Mercedes because the painting doesn't wear out with time.

The art here is from museums, estates, and private collections. This gallery gives you a great chance to see art works that have been buried in private collections and may soon disappear into other ones. The Exchange sells works by "famous" artists and also by the less recognized. Prices are reasonable, so this might be the place to pick up that Motherwell you've always wanted.

A building housing even more galleries is 49 Geary. On the third floor, visit the Stephen Wirtz Gallery, which carries contemporary Californian, American, and European painting, sculpture, and photography. The huge, airy space is well suited to the large works in evidence during my visit.

If you like to look at photos, visit the Fraenkel Gallery on the fourth floor, which devotes itself to 19th and 20th century photography, and is considered one of the premier photo galleries in the country. The gallery displays the work of photographers from 19th century landscape photographer Carleton Watkins to Robert Mapplethorpe. It even displays NASA moon photos!

On the fifth floor is 871 Fine Arts & Bookstore. (The gallery used to be at 871 Folsom, and kept the name.) In addition to art, this store has a

---

[9] If you like installations, visit the Capp Street Project at 525 Second Street (corner of Federal). See "Walk 32" for more information.

A Deborah Butterfield horse in the Bank of America Plaza.

vast collection of out-of-print and hard-to-find find arts books and catalogs. Subjects include painters, sculptors, photographers, and printmakers, with an emphasis on California artists. You can find books on ethnic and outsider—primitive and self-taught—artists.

There are also some pretty nice restrooms on this floor.

Across the street at 14 Geary is the Gallery Paule Anglim, which shows contemporary painting, sculpture, drawing, conceptual art, and video. This gallery handles the big names, but also newcomers and even recent art school graduates. One sculptor they have shown is Deborah Butterfield, whose recent larger-than-life horses look as if they're made of driftwood, but are actually cast in bronze. Two beauties are on display on the Plaza level of the Bank of America, where you started this walk.

GETTING BACK

Walk to the corner of Geary and Kearny. Turn left and continue north on Kearny until you return to the Banker's Heart. Now enter the Bank of America building to look at the Deborah Butterfield horses.

Money Temples—Heart of Downtown

Downtown means banking. As you walk through this area, you will see many old "banking temples," with tall Greek or Roman columns and vast interior banking halls, that do, indeed, have the feel of a hallowed place. I'm not sure whether the idea behind the "temple" architecture was to inspire you to worship money or to make you feel that your money was safe in such a sacrosanct place.

Today, many of the banking temples have been modified—the interior halls broken into offices, and the exteriors built into the sides of larger skyscrapers. However, many of the original features still remain.

This walk is a good chance to brush up on your Greek and Roman columns: Doric, Ionic (the most popular), Corinthian, and Tuscan. They are all here.

I point out some of these banking temples, but you will see many more as you walk along. Downtown has many other fascinating buildings worth looking at, as well.

WALKING TIME

About 35 minutes, not counting time spent exploring the inside of the buildings.

GETTING THERE

You are already there. The Banker's Heart at Bank of America's World Headquarters is the very heart of downtown.

DOWNTOWN

The burnished red-brown surface of Bank of America World Headquarters building (555 California) rises 52 stories into the downtown sky. It is not the tallest building in San Francisco—the

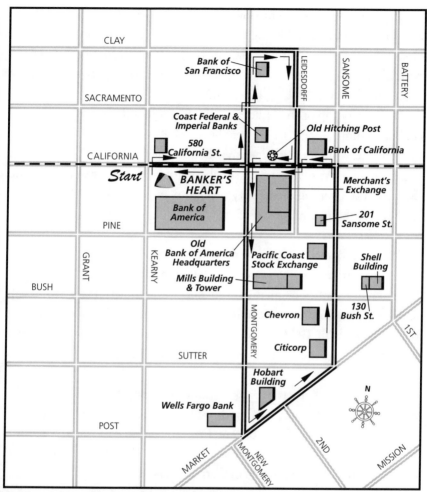

Money Temples - Heart of Downtown

Transamerica Pyramid carries that honor—but it is probably the most massive.

Made of polished carnelian granite from South Dakota, this building changes with the changing hours. Sometimes it looks heavy and somber, at other times radiant with light. Considering its enormous mass, the structure soars with surprising grace.

The World Headquarters building, completed in 1971, contains a staggering 1.8 million feet of office space. Inside are three art galleries: On the Plaza level you can see work mostly by local artists. On the

Concourse level, one flight down, are the Concourse Gallery and the A.P. Giannini Gallery. During the United Nations 50th anniversary celebration, the A.P. Giannini Gallery hosted a retrospective by famous portrait photographer Yousuf Karsh. My favorite portrait: grumpy Winston Churchill looking like a bulldog.

At the very top of the building is the Carnelian Room restaurant and cocktail lounge, open to the public in the evenings and for Sunday brunch. The restaurant is expensive, but the view is the most inspiring in San Francisco. At night, as you see the lights of the city sparkling in the distance, the evening seems very special indeed. I took my dad here for his 80th birthday and for his 85th, and I'm planning to take him again for his 90th.

From the Banker's Heart, walk east one block to Montgomery, and then turn left (north) to view some banking temples. At the corner of Montgomery and Sacramento (456–460 Montgomery), are two small temples built right into a gleaming 24-story high-rise. The Coast Federal Bank was built in 1908 as the Italian-American Bank. The other little temple, the Imperial Bank, was also built in 1908, as the Anton Borel Bank.

Continue north to the Bank of San Francisco (550 Montgomery), now a National Historic Landmark. This was once the Bank of Italy, the forerunner of today's Bank of America. You must go inside to see the sumptuous banking hall, the old, exquisitely detailed bronze tellers' cages, and the gleaming floors of Carrara marble.

Italian American A.P. Giannini started the Bank of Italy at Columbus and Washington Streets in 1904, intending to create a bank where even poor people would have access to banking services. Nine days after the quake and fire, Giannini was outside doing business on a bench, providing bank loans for San Franciscans eager to rebuild. On August 17, 1908, the Bank of Italy opened its new headquarters at 550 California. In 1930, the Bank of Italy became the Bank of America, today one of the world's banking colossuses. The site at 550 Montgomery, currently leased by the Bank of San Francisco, received Landmark status in 1982.

At Clay, turn right and then right again into narrow Leidesdorff. Walk back along this tiny street to California. Near some hitching posts on the corner of Sacramento and Leidesdorff, you will see a plaque commemorating William Alexander Leidesdorff as "builder, entrepreneur, visionary, pioneer, San Franciscan, African-American."

Born in the Virgin Islands in 1810 to a Danish father and a Creole mother, Leidesdorff had an astonishing career. He worked in New Orleans as a cotton broker, captained a ship carrying goods from the Sandwich Islands to San Francisco (then Yerba Buena), served as vice counsel of Mexican Yerba Buena, served as chairman of the schoolboard that built the first public school in San Francisco, and was San Francisco's first city treasurer. After the war with Mexico, he posted the proclamation declaring California part of the United States. Leidesdorff died of typhus in 1848 and is buried at Mission Dolores.

Narrow Leidesdorff was the first San Francisco street created on landfill. Today, except for the plaque, you will see no evidence of William Leidesdorff and his colorful career as you walk down this alley filled with San Franciscans peacefully dining at outdoor tables.

At California, turn right to return to Montgomery. Across from Wells Fargo's Express Stop (464 California), near the curb, is an old hitching post with a lock on it. The interior space was once filled with horse feed. At Montgomery, turn left and walk to the lovely Mills Building (220 Montgomery), which looks like it is made of wet sand. Look up at the huge arch over the entrance, and then go inside to explore the beautiful interior marble court, which today houses art exhibits.

The original structure was built in 1891 by Darius Ogden Mills, who founded the Bank of California, and the Sierra Club was incorporated here the next year. Many famous San Francisco architects have had a hand in this building: Willis Polk was involved in the post-fire 1908 reconstruction and Lewis P. Hobart in the 1931 Mills Tower addition, which opens onto Bush Street.

Cross Montgomery and head south. Just before Market, look up to the east for a wonderful view of the ornate and fantastical Hobart Building tower (582 Market).

At One Montgomery is another banking temple, today owned by Wells Fargo. Crocker Bank, the former owners, developed the public garden on the roof, which you enter from the Crocker Galleria (see

The Hobart Building

"Walk 14"). Designed by Willis Polk in 1908, the temple has a huge and elegant banking hall, which has been preserved. Walk inside to get the feeling of grandeur.

Turn left on Market and walk one block to the corner of Sansome. Here at the corner of Sutter and Sansome is the Citicorp Center (1 Sansome) banking temple, which is set into a large, modern tower. The enclosed plaza with fountain, tables, chairs, and trees rising from a white marble floor is an excellent place to eat your lunch. The statue, *The Star Girl*, was sculpted by Alexander Stirling Calder for the 1915 Panama Pacific International Exposition, which commemorated the completion of the Panama Canal.

Also at this corner, on Sansome, is a fabulous newsstand that carries papers in all languages and from many U.S. cities. If you have a yen to read the *Tampa Tribune* or the *Charlotte Observer*, you can get it here. There are all political persuasions represented too, from the extreme right to the *Revolutionary Worker*.

On Sansome, walk north one block to Bush. In both directions are a number of buildings worth looking at. To the right is my favorite—the ultra-skinny skyscraper at 130 Bush. Only 20 feet wide, this 1910 structure designed by George Applegarth looks like it's plugging an alley, but it's not. There's no lobby. You walk straight from the street into the elevator!

Next to the skinny skyscraper is the 1929 Shell Building (100 Bush) designed by George Kelham. On the left side of Sansome at 225 Bush is another George Kelham building, the 1922 Italian Renaissance Chevron building, formerly the headquarters of Standard Oil of California. Across the street is the Bush entrance to Mills Tower.

Continue north on Sansome past the Royal Insurance building (201 Sansome). Look inside to see the Marble doorways from the Torlonia Palace in Rome. At 155 Sansome is the City Club, a 12-story office tower that stands behind the Pacific Coast Stock Exchange. The lobby is luxurious in black marble and gold leaf. However, the club's most interesting attraction, a large Diego Rivera mural, is in a part of the building not open to the public.

At the corner of Pine and Sansome is a money temple *par excellence*, the Pacific Coast Stock Exchange. Sadly, a posted sign warns "We regret we are closed to the public," so you can't wander in and see the stock-market bustle. As if to retaliate, the public seems to have taken residence on the steps, reading books and newspapers, chatting, and eating lunch. Huge, somewhat stiff 1930s statues by Ralph Stackpole flank the steps: *Mother Earth* and *Man and His Inventions*.

Continue on Sansome to California and cross. You will be in front of the Bank of California at 400 California. This 1907 building by Bliss & Faville, with its Corinthian columns, its 60-foot-high ceilings, and its Tennessee marble interior, is the king of banking temples. The lions that flank the clock were sculpted by Arthur Putnam, a famous California animal sculptor of that era. Built around the temple is the 1967 high-rise tower that contains the bank's offices.

Inside and down the steps is a wonderful exhibit called "Museum of the Money of the American West." If you like to see gold, visit here. You can wander alone (I didn't even see a guard) through gold nuggets, ingots, and coins from California's pre-Mint days. There is also coinage from other Western states such as Colorado and Utah. I found especially fascinating the ornate dueling pistols from the fatal duel between David C. Broderick, an anti-slavery senator from California, and his rival, pro-slavery David S. Terry.

Across California is the Merchant's Exchange (465 California) designed by architect Willis Polk, built in 1903, and rebuilt in 1906 after the quake and fire. Inside is an opulent skylit marble lobby, at the end of which is the Grain Exchange Hall, at one time the financial hub of the

The faceless ladies atop 580 California

city. Here, ship arrivals and departures were monitored, and merchants, shippers, and traders gathered to wheel and deal. Past the four giant columns at the Hall's entrance are some large oil paintings by William A. Coulter showing San Francisco's seafaring history. Sadly, the Grain Exchange Hall was closed to the public at the time of this writing. After First Interstate Bank (the previous tenant) was sold to Wells Fargo, the Grain Exchange Hall had locked glass doors placed across its entrance, with most of the art out of public view.

Right next to the Merchant's Exchange is another banking temple, the old Bank of America headquarters (485 California/300 Montgomery). Designed in 1922 by George Kelham as a "Roman basilica" for the American National Bank, the remodeled building became the headquarters of the Bank of America in 1941. You can't walk inside the California Street part now, but you can peer through the entrance at the strange imitation marble columns.

Walk one block up California back to the Banker's Heart and look across the street at 580 California. On the top of this 23-story building are some truly grisly faceless statues. This 1983 structure was designed by architect Philip Johnson and John Burgee, who also designed the Neiman-Marcus store at Union Square. The statues are by Muriel Castanis. Was the sculptor playing a joke on the city? Look, and decide for yourself.

Two Chinatown Streets— Stockton & Grant

The Chinese community has had some tough times in San Francisco, but right now it's thriving. To see this for yourself, you need only walk through its bustling streets and look at the grandparents pulled along by rosy-cheeked grandchildren, the busy shoppers picking out the freshest produce in overflowing shops, and the tourists elbowing their way through the crowds. This is not to say that problems don't remain, but compared with other inner-city areas, with their boarded-up storefronts and urban decay, Chinatown is flourishing.

The Chinese arrived in San Francisco in sizable numbers during the Gold Rush, when they settled around Portsmouth Square. By 1850, the Chinese community (mostly men) numbered around 4,000. Organized into clans, the Chinese labored in restaurants and laundries, made clothing, cigars, and shoes, and worked in the import/export business and in the fish industry.

At first the Chinese were welcomed. In fact, on August 28, 1850, a celebration was held in Portsmouth Square in honor of the community's Chinese residents. As the flush days of the Gold Rush receded, however, anti-Chinese sentiment grew, increasing even more in the 1870s when Chinese came to the United States in increasing numbers to work on the Southern Pacific Railroad.

As the depression of the 1870s deepened, other San Franciscans blamed Chinese immigrants for the declining wages and hard times. Sandlot orator Denis Kearney, a drayman, further rabble-roused San Franciscans. His political movement, the Workingmen's Party, had as its slogan "The Chinese Must Go." Chinese were beaten, robbed, and even murdered, their restaurants and laundries burned down.

Ultimately, this anti-Chinese feeling led to the passage of the Chinese Exclusion Act of 1882, which ended Chinese immigration for the next

61 years, making it impossible for Chinese men already living here to bring over their wives. The Exclusion Act was repealed in 1943, as a result of the World War II alliance between China and the U.S., but still only a meager 105 Chinese immigrants a year were permitted into the country. It was not until 1965 that President Lyndon Johnson signed a new immigration law, allowing Chinese to enter the country in more significant numbers.

In 1905, the San Francisco Board of Supervisors had the "brilliant" idea of moving Chinatown to Hunters Point. To ensure that this didn't happen, Chinatown leaders rushed to rebuild after the '06 quake right where they were and also to put a unmistakable Chinese stamp on their buildings. Two building that were constructed to "mark" Chinatown at its present location are the Sing Fat and Sing Chong buildings on the corners of Grant and California. This blend of local San Francisco architecture adorned with Chinese motifs—pagodas, ornate balconies and cornices, curved eaves—is called *chinoiserie*.

I like to think of Stockton as the "real" Chinatown and Grant as the "tourist" Chinatown. However, as with most generalizations, there are countless exceptions: there are lots of tourist spots on Stockton and lots of authentic Chinatown on Grant.

WALKING TIME

About 45 minutes, not counting detours into side streets and alleys. However, this time estimate is not very meaningful, as the streets are so crowded at noon that most of the time, you're just inching along.

GETTING THERE

From the Banker's Heart at Kearny and California, head north on Kearny to Sacramento. Then turn left. You are already in Chinatown, which, after all, has no distinct borders. On the south side of the street (755-65 Sacramento), notice the Nam Kue school with its elaborate front courtyard. Opened in 1920 and at its present location since 1925, this little school provides instruction in Chinese language, history, and culture to schoolchildren in the community. To accommodate the regular school schedule, Nam Kue is open in the late afternoon and on Saturdays.

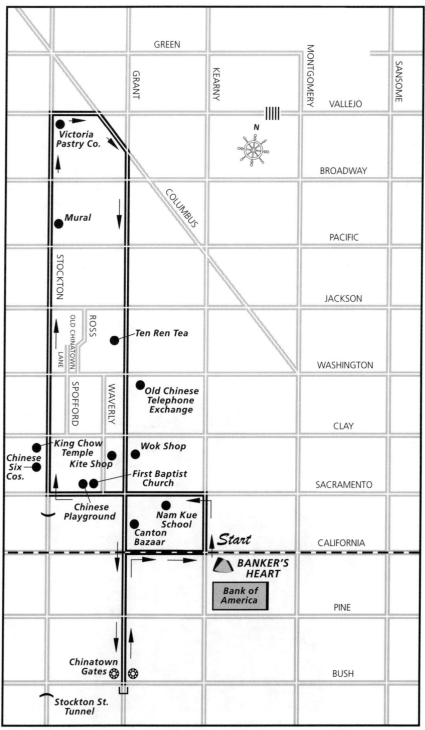

Two Chinatown Streets: Stockton and Grant

It's hard to believe but at one time, Chinese children were prohibited from attending public schools. It was not until a lawsuit in 1885 (Mamie Tape vs. Jean Hurley, principal) that schools—strictly segregated—were established for Chinese children.

On the north side of the street, at the corner of Waverly and Sacramento, is the dark clinker brick First Chinese Baptist Church, which has been at this site since 1888. This ancient-looking, now-boarded-up structure was built in 1908, to replace the one that tumbled during the '06 quake. The church, like many others, offered education to both adults and children in the community.

Just past the Church is the Chinese Playground with its many play structures and children crowded into a tiny space.

Just before you get to Stockton, you will see a little street on the left called *Brooklyn*. Hey, what's this doing here!

The boarded up First Chinese Baptist Church

STOCKTON STREET

When you get to Stockton, look to your left to see the entrance to the Stockton Street tunnel. The arch of the tunnel was created in 1914 as part of Mayor James Rolph, Jr's "City Beautiful" movement, but today, choked with cars and buses, the arch and the tunnel don't seem all that special.

Turn right and start walking up Stockton. I always like to just submerge myself in the atmosphere of this wonderful and varied street, rather than focusing on buildings, but there are a few you should notice. On the west side of the street is the elaborate Chinese Six Companies building.[10] Notice the two lions guarding the entrance. This intricate building was partly constructed with forty thousand taels of silver sent to Chinatown by the Imperial Court after the '06 quake. It is one of Chinatown's most colorful buildings—brilliant red, yellow, green, and sky blue.

Just to the north , at the corner of Clay and Stockton, is the elaborate Kong Chow Temple. The actual temple is on the top floor; below is a U.S. Post Office.

Now cross Washington and forget about buildings. This section of Stockton is about food. The streets are absolutely jammed with Chinese shoppers, and your stroll will slow to a bare shuffle, or perhaps stop altogether. Being a "type A" New Yorker, I have occasionally given up on the sidewalks entirely and walked down the street.

Here are overflowing vegetable markets, butcher shops, fish stores, bakeries. Barbecued ducks hang in windows; fish swim in tanks. Everything looks perfectly fresh. There are also trading companies, where, often, I can't identify the products at all. In one such store, all I could recognize were peanuts!

I have never been able to walk through this part of Chinatown without buying something. Last time it was dried sweet potatoes.

---

[10] The Chinese Six Companies is an influential benevolent association made up of members from the six districts of China. Formed around 1862, it has provided help to Chinese immigrants, lobbied against discrimination, and even administered justice within the Chinese community.

Recently, in San Francisco, there has been a big flap about selling live animals—such as fish and turtles—for food, a common practice in Stockton's Chinatown markets. In fact, as of the time of this writing, animal-rights activists are suing about a dozen Asian-owned markets, claiming cruelty to animals. The merchants have responded that live-animal markets are part of the community's tradition and ensure that the food is fresh.

As you pass Jackson, look at the gigantic community mural painted on the wall of the Ping Yuen apartments. Holes are left in the mural for tenants' windows.

Although Broadway is the "official" end of Chinatown, continue to Vallejo. Between Broadway and Vallejo is Mee Mee Fortune Cookies (1328 Stockton), where you can get custom-made fortune cookies. Yes, this means what you think it does.

Continue to the corner of Broadway and Vallejo, where you will come to the incomparable Victoria Pastry Company, famous for its Saint Honoré cake, a blend of pastry, custard, chocolate, lemon custard, rum-soaked cake, and whipped cream. To me, Victoria's is the end of Chinatown and the beginning of North Beach. Now, to get a quick breather from the crowds, turn right to Columbus. Walk down Columbus to Broadway; then plunge back into the maelstrom by continuing south on Grant.

GRANT AVENUE

Grant Avenue is San Francisco's first street. Originally a dirt road called Calle de La Fundacion, the street was renamed Dupont Street in 1846 after Naval Commander Samuel F. Dupont. It was infamous for its brothels, gambling and opium dens, and vice of all kinds. After the '06 quake and fire destroyed Dupont, community leaders were determined to improve Dupont's image, and they renamed the street after the Ulysses S. Grant. Why is Grant an "avenue," when all the parallel streets are just plain "streets?" I don't know.

If Stockton is about food, Grant is about goods, which range from cheap souvenirs—tinny models of the Golden Gate Bridge—to exquisite imported jade, porcelain, silks, gold jewelry, oriental carpets, cloisonné, and, yes, ivory. There are also great restaurants here, my favorite being Kowloon, the tiny, inexpensive vegetarian restaurant at 909 Grant. Grant is also about a jumble of people—Chinatown residents, tourists, business people, kids, grandparents—all peacefully jostling together as they make their way—very slowly—down the street.

A few places stand out.

Between Jackson and Washington is Grand Jewelry (955 Grant), occupying what probably is San Francisco's narrowest building. It is only six feet ten inches wide, and may be plugging up what once was an alley. The gold sold here, as in the rest of Chinatown, is a yellower gold than you will see sold in other parts of the city.

A little further along is the Ten Ren Tea Company (949 Grant), where you can get a break from the crowd and shop for fine teas. I saw one green tea selling for $93.80 a pound and couldn't resist buying my husband a quarter of a pound. He's aging it a bit before he tries it, so I can't give you the verdict yet. (As a sign of the times, Ten Ren also has a very professionally designed Web site at http://www.tenren.com.)

Looking south on Grant

When you get to Washington, cross and detour slightly to the east to look at the bright green and red Bank of Canton (743 Washington) with its ultra fancy three-tiered pagoda. This is the site of the Old Chinese Telephone Exchange, America's only Chinese telephone exchange. San Francisco's first newspaper, the *California Star*, was also published here.

In the 1880s, many Chinese merchants were labor contractors who organized Chinese work crews. The merchants originally installed a phone in a building at Washington and Grant (then Dupont) to receive calls from those wanting to hire the workers. At first, children were hired as messengers to run and tell people they had a call. With business booming, the phone company purchased the site at 743 Washington and built its own building. At this time, all the phone operators were men. In 1909, after the quake, the Exchange was rebuilt in "Chinese" style and staffed with female operators, who had to be proficient in many Chinese

The Sing Chong building at California and Grant

dialects. In the 1950s, the Bank of Canton purchased the building, preserving the exterior as an historic site.

Between Clay and Sacramento is the Wok Shop (718 Grant). where you can buy everything you could possibly need for Chinese cooking. The store also has linens, hanging lanterns, and, in a bow to the tourist trade, tee shirts. Across the street, the Kite Shop (717 Grant) is a good place to browse and perhaps buy a hand-painted kite. Some are just ornamental, so check out what you buy.

At the corner of Grant and Sacramento is a Bank of America branch (701 Grant). It's only two blocks from the towering Bank of America World Headquarters (home of the Banker's Heart), but, architecturally, the branch—with its gold dragon medallions and ornate red columns—is a world away.

Continue south to the Canton Bazaar at 616 Grant. This is a store that is *filled* with statues, urns, candelabra, teak furniture, jewelry boxes, fans, parasols, beads, silks, and anything else you can think of. It's really hopping in here. If you need a rest, stop in next door, at the peaceful Paulist Center—the bookstore of Old St. Mary's Cathedral. Here you can listen to soothing liturgical music while you browse the bookshelves. *Twelve Months of Monastery Soups* caught my eye.

On the corners of California and Grant are the pagoda-topped Sing Fat and Sing Chong buildings. With its pagoda above and its McDonalds below, the Sing Chong building seems to symbolize the mixture of styles and cultures that define Chinatown.

South of Pine, the tourist shops seem more filled with junky souvenirs—more dancing figurines and cheap plaster models of the Last Supper. More non-Chinatown shops—discount shoes and cameras—too. You know for sure you're exiting Chinatown, however, when you come to the Sabra (419 Grant), a strictly kosher Jewish restaurant.

At Grant and Bush is the Chinatown Gate, which marks the southern border of Chinatown. Built in 1970, this triple-portaled gate leads you into Chinatown and Grant Avenue. Notice the fierce mystical dogs on either side of the gate, guarding it. The sign hanging in the center translates to "All Under Heaven is Good for the People." It is a saying of Dr. Sun Yat-sen.

SIDE STREETS

Of course, stitching Grant and Stockton together are wonderful side streets. Best for exploring is Washington, which offers its *own* wonderful side streets. Washington, between Grant and Stockton, has four such streets, each with its own character, and each worth visiting.

Running north is Old Chinatown Lane, narrow and mysterious. Here are a number of dismal-looking "sewing companies," with covered-over windows. Not a good sign. A barber shop offers haircuts for five dollars. Also running north is lively Ross Alley, home to jewelry shops, the exotic Sam Bo Trading Company, and the tiny Golden Gate Fortune Cookie Company.

Running south is Spofford, as narrow as Old Chinatown Lane and home to more sewing companies. There's some history in this alley, too. At 36 Spofford is the headquarters of the Chee Kung Tong, a secret society that dates back to the 1850s. In 1904, Dr. Sun Yat-sen stayed here for about six years, writing and working to overthrow the Manchu Dynasty and promote democracy.

Also running south from Washington is glamorous Waverly Place with its colorful painted balconies. Waverly is also home to several temples, which you can visit. There is the Tin How Temple (123-29 Waverly) and the Norras Temple (109-11 Waverly). The painted balconies are almost all on the west side of the street, so walk down the east side for the best view.

GETTING BACK

From the Chinatown Gate, walk north on Grant to California. Then turn right and walk one block to return to the Banker's Heart.

Pier 39 & the Sea Lions WALK 21

This walk is a long leg-stretcher that will take you through quintessential San Francisco with its churches, outdoor cafés, eateries, Broadway sex shows, parks, hills, views, residential areas, and tourist spots.

WALKING TIME

A little over an hour if you walk at a brisk clip. Add about 15 minutes if you return via Grant Avenue and climb up to Jack Early Park.

GETTING THERE

This is a walk whose purpose is the walking itself, not just the goal, so look around you as you go. From the Banker's Heart at California and Kearny head north on Kearny and then turn left (northwest) on Columbus. Make sure to look at copper-green Columbus Tower at the corner of Kearny and Columbus (906 Kearny). Also called the Sentinel Building, this flatiron structure, was built just around the time of the great quake and fire, which it mostly survived. In the '70s, the building was purchased by Francis Ford Coppola, who restored it. (For the record, a "flatiron" building is a wedge-shaped building usually built in the space left where two streets join at a sharp angle, like this building at Columbus and Kearny or like the Flood Building at Powell and Market. The most famous is the Flatiron Building in New York on 5th Avenue.)

Continue up Columbus, past Vesuvio's and the City Lights Bookstore (subject of "Walk 13"), past the Broadway sex clubs, past the Stinking Rose garlic restaurant, and into the heart of North Beach. For a great take-out sandwich, stop at Molinari's Deli at Columbus and Vallejo (373 Columbus). The fabulous aroma alone is worth stopping for. Since I'm a vegetarian, I always get Joe's special with its fat little mozzarella balls and

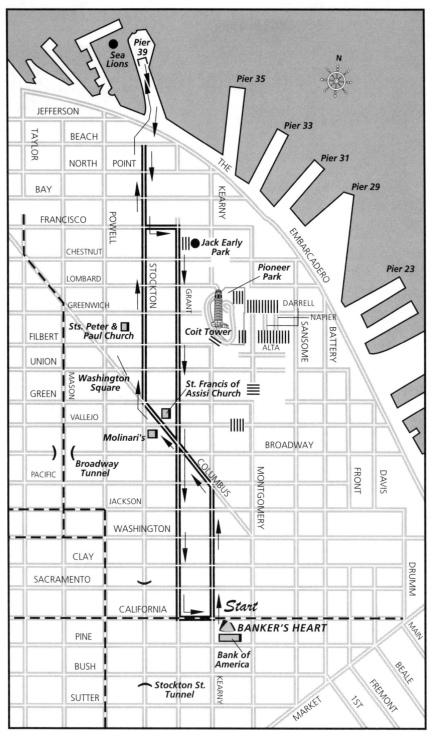

Pier 39 and the Sea Lions

marinated peppers. I know those mozzarella balls are pure artery clog, but the sandwich is irresistible.

Turning to more spiritual matters, cross Columbus to see St. Francis of Assisi, a pretty Catholic church that dates from the Gold-Rush era. As you cross Columbus from Molinari's, look straight down the middle of the street for a perfect view of the Transamerica Pyramid. (Please be careful; there's lots of traffic here.)

Continue on Columbus to Stockton and turn right (north). You will soon see Washington Square on your left, a good spot to eat your take-out sandwich. Like most other downtown parks, Washington Square is host to a varied clientele—the homeless, working people eating lunch, retired people, and children playing in the sandbox. Unlike Portsmouth Square and St. Mary's, Washington Square escaped the humiliation of becoming the roof of a parking garage. Note the fancy Sts. Peter and Paul Church on the north edge of the Square. Dedicated in 1924, the church is run by the Salesian Order of St. John Bosco, the patron saint of poor youth. It appeared in the Cecil B. DeMille movie *The Ten Commandments.*

Continue on Stockton for the last leg of this walk—actually my favorite part. From Greenwich on, you view the Bay as you stroll through this ordinary San Francisco neighborhood. Not quite North Beach, not quite Telegraph Hill, not quite Fisherman's Wharf, second fiddle to more colorful Grant Avenue, this residential section of Stockton is lined with typical San Francisco houses and is incredibly pleasant to walk through. It's bay windows solid from Filbert to Bay.

Cross the Embarcadero to arrive at Pier 39.

PIER 39

Pier 39 is too touristy to criticize for being touristy. Actually, the woody gray two-level structure with its many offbeat shops gives Pier 39 a unique, rather than a cookie-cutter, feel. Since it opened in October of 1978, Pier 39 has become San Francisco's most popular attraction, hosting over 10 million visitors a year.

As you walk through, you will see shops that sell pearls, fancy boxes, goods for left-handed people, shells, socks, puppets, kites, posters

The sea lions lounging at Pier 39: K dock

"Victorian" goods (whatever these are) , and an open-air fruit market that offers a fountain for washing fruit—very California. My favorite shop is Wound About, which is exclusively devoted to wind-up toys and seems like something I dreamed about long ago. There are also pricey restaurants and clean, free restrooms.

Walk past the Venetian carousel and the stage with its magic shows until you come to the water. Take in the sobering view of Alcatraz. You can see why people called this prison "the rock." Bear around to the left to view the sea lions.

Ah, the sea lions. What are they doing in the city at noon? Who brought them? Who makes them stay? The answer is this: They came to the "K" dock unbidden around 1990 and at first were considered a major nuisance. They honked; they stank; they refused to charge admission. The powers that be nefariously plotted to get rid of them. But one day, these same powers realized that the pesky sea lions had quietly become Pier 39's biggest attraction and that tourists were flocking to see them. So the sea lions were left alone.

On weekends, the Marine Mammal Center offers free talks about these creatures right at the Pier. Note that most of the seal lions migrate south around June, so don't count on seeing them during the summer months.

It's fun to stand by the railing and watch them shoving one another off the floating docks or to just enjoy them lazing in the sun. Whenever I watch them snoozing and playing, I always think about the afternoon's work ahead of me at my high-pressured tech-writing job and wonder if it's so important after all.

GETTING BACK

I like to go back the same way I came because there's so much to see. For variety, I just walk on the other side of the street.

But if you want a lot more variety and also a hillier walk, cut over to Grant Avenue (one block left) at Francisco and continue on Grant all the way back. Then, at California, turn left to return to Banker's Heart. This will take you past the upscale part of upper Grant, through the center of North Beach, and into Chinatown.

If you take the Grant Avenue detour, make sure to visit minuscule Jack Early Park on Grant between Francisco and Chestnut on the east side of the street. This "park" actually consists of two tiny one-seater benches at the top of a steep stairway. It's secluded, romantic, and offers a magnificent view of the Bay from bridge to bridge.

An Aerobic Tramp on San Francisco's Long Trail—The Filbert & Greenwich Steps

If you've ever vacationed in Vermont and walked the Long Trail, you know that it's full of narrow paths, steep ups and downs, hidden surprises, sudden vistas, terrain changes, steps, and even ladders to get you across a few really difficult places. The San Francisco version doesn't have any ladders, but it has all the other features, including plenty of steps.

This walk is hard on knees, so if your knees are already hurting, *don't do this walk until they've recovered.* I once did the walk when I was having knee problems, and my knees were history by the time I was done. Then, because I don't have much sense, I did it again the next week so I could smell the fennel once more. And now? Let's just say I ended up doing my leg lifts faithfully every day.

WALKING TIME

Allow about 70 minutes for the walk. If you plan on taking the Alta Street extension stroll, add another 10 minutes.

GETTING THERE

There are many enjoyable routes from the Banker's Heart to the steps and back. Try a couple of different ways. This is my favorite route:

From the Banker's Heart on Kearny and California, walk east one block to Montgomery. Then walk straight north on Montgomery, past the pointy Transamerica building, past the designer showrooms and interior decorator houses, past the Broadway honky tonks until you get to Vallejo Street. Turn around to view the Bay Bridge, looking uncharacteristically glamorous from this angle. (This view did not exist before the demolition of the Embarcadero Freeway.)

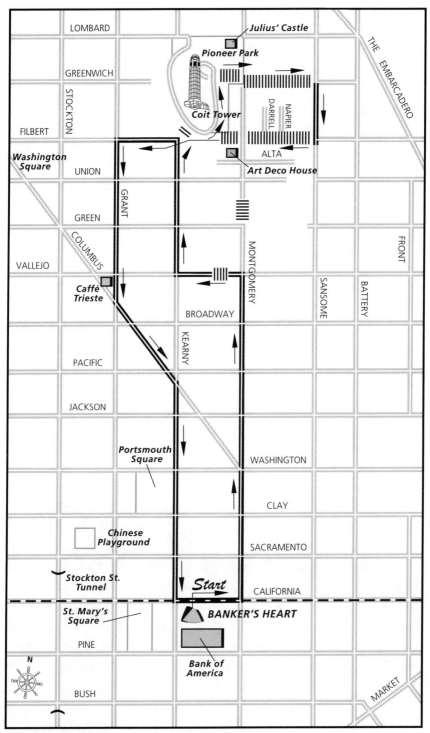

**An Aerobic Tramp on San Francisco's Long Trail --
The Filbert and Greenwich Steps**

Turn left on Vallejo and you will walk up an elegant flight of steps and then back down to Kearny street. Beautiful plants, maintained by the Department of Urban Forestry, adorn this stairway. In the summer, giant sprays of sunflowers will cheer you on.

Now, turn right and walk straight up Kearny until it ends (temporarily) at Filbert. The last block (from Union to Filbert) is *really* steep. The writer Richard Brautigan, author of *Trout Fishing in America*, lived at 1425 Kearny during the late '60s. He probably pounded away at his typewriter all day because going anywhere was too exhausting.

On Filbert, walk up the steps to Telegraph Hill Boulevard and Coit Tower. Circle to the right around the Boulevard until you get to the Greenwich Street sign at the light pole.

But before you descend, take a moment to walk to the lookout just past the statue of Christopher Columbus. Here you will enjoy the panoramic view that San Franciscans in the Gold Rush era relished as they watched for approaching ships carrying hungered-after mail, news, and goods. The lookout's semaphore (a signaling system using flags on arm-like projections) was built in 1849 and replaced in 1853 by California's first electric telegraph system, hence the name "Telegraph Hill."

Take another few minutes to walk into Coit Tower itself, and view the Depression-era frescoes inside. Commissioned in 1934 by the Works Progress Administration (WPA), the murals provided work for unemployed local artists. The frescoes, painted in the style of Mexican painter Diego Rivera (who had taught several of the muralists), show scenes of Californians at work.

Completed just as the bloody 1934 Waterfront Strike exploded, the murals, with their socialist-realist themes, were considered subversive, and the opening of Coit Tower was delayed to avoid displaying them. Before the tower was permitted to open, a mural by artist Clifford Wight was altered to remove a piece of wire shaped like a hammer and sickle and also to paint out the words "United Workers of the World."

THE GREENWICH STEPS

Start descending the brick steps down to the Julius' Castle restaurant. Note the beautifully maintained gardens on each side. (Stay on the brick; don't veer off on the cement lane, which will lead you to the Filbert Steps one block south).

Continue down until you reach Montgomery Street. Then, cross Montgomery Street and turn around to look back at Julius' Castle (1541 Montgomery). At first it seems as if the steps have ended, but if you walk south on Montgomery (away from the restaurant) until you come to the Greenwich Street sign, you will see the continuation. Keep going down.

This section of the Greenwich Steps is concrete. In contrast to the Filbert-step gardens, which you will soon see, the foliage here looks wild—lots of fuchsias and ferns that seem to be gardening themselves. Toward the bottom, the smell of fennel is strong.

Today, the little secluded houses straddling the steps are trendy, but 100 years ago, the hill was occupied by poor Irish immigrants who worked on the piers below. To them, dragging groceries and supplies up and down the precarious trails might not have seemed like that much fun.

Early in this century, the hill became a hangout for artists and writers, attracted by the inexpensive living, access to cafes and bars, great views,

Photo by Jacquelyne Cordes

Mark Bittner and his wild parrots

and generally funky atmosphere. Today, the hill is no longer inexpensive, but it's still funky.

When I recently walked here with my husband Pete, about half way down the steps a thrilling flock of wild parrots swirled around us. The feeder of the parrots, a Telegraph Hill denizen named Mark Bittner, told us that the flock consists of cherry-headed conures except for a single mitred conure and a single blue conure. All from Ecuador.

Alas, the parrots don't appear on a regular schedule for their sunflower seeds, so you may have to go back many times before you see them.

When you get to the bottom of the steps, walk south one block to Filbert Street. You are walking through Levi's Plaza (subject of "Walk 8"). Look upward to view Telegraph Hill's rugged east slope. During the 19th century, some of the hill was dynamited and used for ships' ballast and also for Bay fill.

THE FILBERT STEPS

At Filbert, look toward the hill to see the Filbert Steps. These are better known than the Greenwich Steps because of the efforts of Grace Marchant, who is responsible for the magnificent gardens that adorn the

Looking up at the Filbert Steps

pretty Victorian cottages along the way. In 1949 when she was 63, Marchant moved to then-garbage-strewn Telegraph Hill. A former dock-yard worker and Hollywood stuntswoman, she set about single-handedly cleaning up the hill. The story goes that at first she just hurled trash over the cliff's edge, but later got the city's permission to burn the accumulated garbage in a giant bonfire that lasted three days and nights. After cleaning up the hill, Marchant straightaway began planting, and it is the descendants of these early plantings that have grown into the present beautiful stairway gardens at the upper part of the Filbert Steps. Near the top, look for the plaque commemorating her efforts.

The first part of the steps is actually a concrete stairway built over a former rock quarry. Here the greenery is still untamed, with nasturtium and fennel growing wild over the rock. You may see some wild cats roaming around. Actually, Telegraph hill is pretty well covered with cats.

You will soon come to a little bench, after which the steps turn to wood and seem somewhat rickety. But as the steps become more primitive, the plantings become more cultivated. Here you can see the fruit of Grace Marchant's efforts. Turn around now and then to view the Bay.

Walk down tiny Napier Lane (actually a boardwalk of wooden planks) and look at the cottages. Legend says that sailors "shanghaied" in San Francisco were kept in some of the early Napier Lane cottages.

Keep plodding upward until you get to Montgomery Street. You'll be in a sweat. At 1360 Montgomery (corner of Filbert), you can see the Art Deco building that is supposed to look like a ship (not to me, it doesn't). Remodeled in 1939 by Irvin Goldstine, the building was made famous by the Humphrey Bogart/Lauren Bacall movie *Dark Passage*.

If you have time for a horizontal cool-down, you can turn left (south) on Montgomery to Alta Street. When you get to Alta, turn left again and walk to the end, looking at the mixture of old and new houses and listening to the Italian opera that occasionally pours from the open windows. On this tiny street lived writer Armistead Maupin, author of *Tales of the City*, which ran as a serial in the *San Francisco Chronicle* in 1976. The book has more recently been made into a PBS series. The view at the end of Alta is spectacular, and if you lean over (carefully), you can see the steps you just walked nestled into the rocky hillside.

Return to the Filbert Steps and climb to the other side of Montgomery, which is on two levels here. If you wish, you can then explore the remaining part of Alta, extending from Montgomery's west side. Then keep hiking up until the steps end at Telegraph Hill Boulevard.

GETTING BACK

Just stay on Filbert and walk down to Grant Avenue. Look at the Golden Gate Bridge and stop thinking about your knees. Walk down Grant through historic North Beach, and, if time permits, stop for coffee at Caffé Trieste[11] (corner of Grant and Vallejo). Opened in 1954, Caffé Trieste is one of the oldest coffee houses on the West Coast. It was a favorite beat poet hangout.

Take Grant to Columbus, and then walk down Columbus to Kearny. Continue south on Kearny to the Banker's Heart.

VARIATIONS

Next time, try some variations. Try walking straight up Montgomery to Telegraph Hill Boulevard. You will climb some interesting steps on Montgomery between Green and Union streets. Or, try going up Kearny all the way. This will take you up the Kearny heart-attack street/steps between Broadway and Vallejo, one of the few San Francisco streets too steep to drive. (Car access to Kearny is blocked by a fence at Vallejo and by a "Do Not Enter" sign at Broadway, although drivers can actually sneak in through a little side street, Fresno. Let's hope their brakes are good.) Or, try going *down* the Filbert Steps and *up* the Greenwich Steps to see different views.

Or, just walk up Grant to the Caffé Trieste, sit down with an espresso, and save the San Francisco Long Trail for another day.

---

[11] The Italian word for café is caffè, but the sign at the Trieste says "caffé," so take your pick.

Heart of North Beach   WALK 23

Everyone loves North Beach with its great bookstores and cafés, sultry bars, intimate Italian restaurants, fragrant bakeries, inspiring churches, funky music, enticing delis, colorful locals, and thrilling views. North Beach has no exact boundaries, blending gradually into Chinatown, the financial district, Telegraph Hill, Fisherman's Wharf, and Russian Hill. You can think of North Beach as a state of mind. If you think you're here, you probably are!

It was once the northern curve of the city and also a beach. But with San Francisco nibbling away at the Bay for a century and a half, the beach is long since gone, so don't expect to come here and dig your toes into the sand. Although today North Beach is considered San Francisco's Italian neighborhood, actually Chileans, Irish, and various Latin Americans arrived first. In fact, Italians didn't arrive in great numbers until the turn of the century. Today Chinatown is expanding northward, and this "Italian" neighborhood is about half Chinese.

North Beach is San Francisco's bohemia, its Left Bank, achieving prominence in the 1950s as the center of beat-generation culture with Lawrence Ferlinghetti, Allen Ginsberg, Jack Kerouac, Kenneth Rexroth, Michael McClure, and Gary Snyder, among others, living—or at least hanging out—here.

The area has an authentic feel; it's a neighborhood that has grown through time and history, evolving and changing. People live and work here—artists, writers, laborers, shopkeepers, toilers in the downtown financial district. It wasn't created in City Hall and popularized through glossy marketing brochures as was San Francisco's South of Market Yerba Buena "neighborhood."

This walk has three parts: the first takes you though Upper Grant to see some quintessential North Beach shops; the second takes you to the little North Beach Museum on Stockton to catch up on some history; the third zigzags through North Beach's streets and alleys so you can see how the denizens live.

WALKING TIME
Between 60 and 75 minutes.

GETTING THERE
From the Banker's Heart at Kearny and California, head north on Kearny. As you walk, more and more Italian restaurants and cafés will appear amidst the many Chinese restaurants and shops.

So where does North Beach start? For me, a good candidate is the giant hole in the ground on the east side of Kearny just before Jackson. This was the site of the International Hotel, torn down in 1977 after years of controversy, litigation, demonstrations, marches, picketing, and arrests. Once serving as home to low-income, elderly Filipino-Americans, the International Hotel found itself caught in the center of an expanding downtown district with its building boom of offices and luxury apartments.

On the Jackson Street side of the same hole was once the original "hungry i" (599 Jackson). It was here that a parade of famous comedians

The new "hungry i" on Broadway

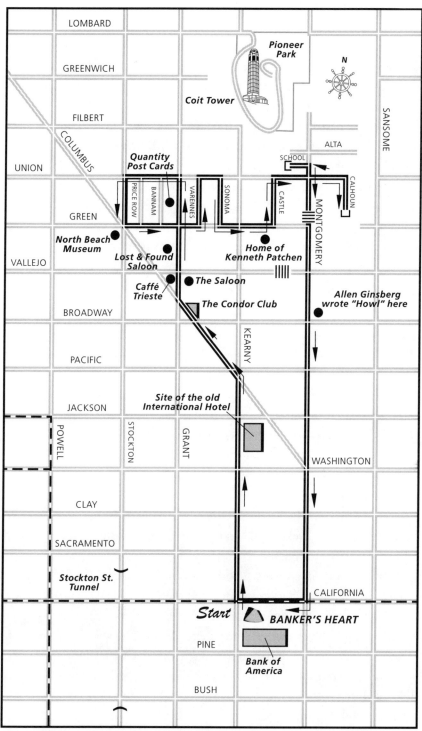

Heart of North Beach

and other nightclub performers got their start. The impressive list of performers includes Mort Sahl, Lenny Bruce, Bill Cosby, Dick Gregory, and even Woody Allen. The current "hungry i" is a Broadway strip joint with no resemblance to the original.

Continue past the hole, and turn left (northwest) on Columbus. As you walk past Tosca's (a venerable old North Beach bar), Vesuvio's, and the City Lights Bookstore (see "Walk 13"), you will have no doubt that you are in North Beach. Cross Broadway and glance at the strip joints. The most famous is the Condor (300 Columbus) where Carol Doda once danced topless on a grand piano. Today, you will see signs offering "lap dancing, wall dancing, couch dancing." I was often a wall "flower," but never a wall dancer. Somehow, I don't think it's the same thing.

Across Broadway, continue on Columbus to Grant.

UPPER GRANT

Upper Grant—from Columbus to Union is the shopping lifeline of North Beach. Two qualities make this street fascinating: first, there are no chain stores—no Burger Kings or Ben Franklin's; every shop is unique. Second, you are strolling through a real neighborhood, so as you walk, you pass not only little Italian restaurants and cafés, but also hardware stores, small groceries and delis, jewelry stores, bakeries, clothing stores, and *lots* of laundromats. I counted two on Grant between Columbus and Union, another one right around the corner on Union, and another two a block further north, between Union and Filbert. Either North Beach residents are the cleanest folks in town or their apartments are too small to hold a washer and dryer.

Here are a couple of my favorite shops: First is the Caffé Trieste at Grant and Vallejo. Serving coffee since 1954, Caffé Trieste is North Beach's linchpin. On Sunday afternoons, local folks gather here to sing opera and whatever else inspires them. What I like best about Caffé Trieste is that you can hunker down at a little table with your espresso and a good book and stay there as long as you want. No one gives you dirty looks or hints that you should move along. The coffee here is *really* strong. Don't say I didn't warn you.

Another favorite is Quantity Post Cards at 1441 Grant between Green and Union. This shop is nostalgia paradise. An assortment of old amusement-park memorabilia and giant paper-maché heads in the window sets the stage. Inside are vintage posts cards of every kind from mawkish valentines to tasteless joke cards. The owner's little dog snuggles in a basket near the cash register. Most cards are only 75 cents and you can browse all day.

There are also two great-looking "saloons" on Grant. I actually haven't been inside of them, but I *have* peeked in. Across from the Caffé Trieste is The Saloon (1232 Grant). This is the site of the longest running drinking establishment in the West. It opened as Wagner's Beer Hall in 1861, and has been quenching thirsts ever since. In the evenings you can dance and listen to rhythm & blues and rock bands.

One block up is the Lost and Found Saloon (1353 Grant), which looks seductively grungy. Here, at the site of the old Coffee Gallery (a beat hangout, where I long ago heard Allen Ginsberg read), are locals hunched over their brew listening to blues and rock music. I'm working up the nerve to walk in.

When you get to Union and Grant, stand on the southeast corner. Look at the gorgeous curbside flowers planted on Union. Gaze at North Beach Pizza and the Italian French Bakery across Grant, and then inhale the salami smells from the Prudente Deli next to you. Now, that's North Beach!

THE NORTH BEACH MUSEUM

To get to the North Beach Museum, walk west on Union to Stockton. Notice the buildings on Union with their typical North Beach architecture—little shops below and bay-windowed dwellings above. Peep down Bannam and Jasper, two of the many neighborhood alleys. North Beach alleys have no bay windows (they were originally forbidden by fire code) and, of course, are much darker, as you can see by the flowers gasping for light in the occasional window boxes.

Turn left at Stockton and continue until you come to the Eureka Bank (1435 Stockton) just south of Green. (You will have to negotiate a messy crossing where Green, Columbus, and Stockton come together.)

The North Beach Museum is on the mezzanine of the Eureka Bank. It's free and open whenever the Bank is. Walk up the narrow steps even if it looks dark upstairs; the museum magically lights up as you enter! Inside is a large framed handwritten poem by Lawrence Ferlinghetti, "The Old Italians Dying."

The exhibits change frequently, so you will see different photographs and artifacts from the ones I saw. I looked at old elementary school desks with ink wells (identical to the ones I used in the Bronx), 19th century hand-embroidered baby bonnets and nightcaps, and lots of photographs of old North Beach. The many pictures of public school children are entirely of boys. Where were the girls? You may see pictures of the earthquake and fire, of Italians and Chinese North Beach immigrants, or of favorite son Joe DiMaggio.

NORTH BEACH DWELLINGS

Now, let's see how the locals live.

After leaving the Museum, walk north a few feet to Green and cross Stockton at the messy intersection. Walk east on Green, a typical North Beach residential street with many light-gathering bay windows. As you walk uphill, the residences get fancier and fancier, as do the alleys, which you will zigzag through.

Past Grant, turn left into Varennes. This little alley can be quite dirty at times, as though all of North Beach's flotsam blew into here. Note that almost all the alley homes have protective window grates, some brightly painted, perhaps to deflect attention from their somber purpose. The alleys and their sidewalks are narrow, and drivers struggle to angle cars into the tiny garages. Often music floods from the grated windows.

Exit Varennes at Union and continue uphill. Then, turn right into Sonoma alley, which, higher on the hill, is a little cleaner and fancier. Notice the many balconies.

Exit Sonoma at Green and continue uphill on Green. After Kearny, Green becomes pretty steep and you will probably be sweating. Look across the street for 377 Green, the home of the late poet and artist Kenneth Patchen and his wife Miriam. Then, turn right into Castle. This

Nineteen century home at
287 Union Street

is the fanciest alley yet—actually fashionable—with brightly painted dwellings and even a few trees leaning toward the alley center trying to get some light. Exit Castle on Union. On the corner of Castle and Union is yet another laundry.

NO PARKING. VISUALIZE BEING TOWED reads the California-style warning at 343 Union. Continue upward. When you get to Montgomery, views of the Bay open around you. On the corner is Speedy's New Union Grocery (301 Union), a corner grocery and neighborhood tradition that dates from the 1920s. It was named for former owners, the Spediacci family.

From here to Calhoun, where Union, ends, you will see some earthquake-surviving 19th century homes. I particularly like the 1860s lavender-gray house at 287 Union with its exterior zigzagged stairs.

Turn right into the upper level of Calhoun, a split-level street that ends with dramatic views of downtown and the Bay. Look straight below and you will realize that you are roosting on the edge of a steep, rocky precipice.

From Calhoun, return to the corner of Union and Montgomery. For a final look at old San Francisco, turn right on Montgomery to School, a tiny, dead-end alley paved with dark brick and lined with impatiens blooming in the dim light. Truly, this transports you to a different era. A little plaque on the house to your right reads "circa 1863."

GETTING BACK

Walk south on Montgomery, down a flight of steps to Green.

Continue south on Montgomery. Just before Broadway you will come to 1010 Montgomery, the house where Allen Ginsberg wrote the first part of *Howl*. It was here he wrote the famous lines, which he first read in the Six Gallery on Fillmore Street on October 13, 1955:

> I saw the best minds of my generation destroyed by
> madness, starving hysterical naked,
> dragging themselves through the negro streets at dawn looking
> for an angry fix[12]

Continue on Montgomery to California. Then turn right to return to the Banker's Heart.

---

[12] Allen Ginsberg. *Howl and Other Poems* (San Francisco: City Lights Books, 1956), p. 9.

Aerobic Walk to Russian Hill South

"I don't see Russians," I said when I first saw Russian Hill in 1965 in the middle of the Cold War. "Where are the Russians?"

According to legend, the hill's name comes from the Russian fur trappers who once voyaged to this coast to hunt sea otter and were later buried on the hilltop, their graves marked with simple black crosses. If the Russians ever were here, however, there's no evidence of them now. As you walk through this residential neighborhood, you will not see any graves, foreign or local.

Unlike Nob Hill, which has always catered to the "upper crust," Russian Hill has sheltered many artists and writers, including Ina Donna Coolbrith, Jack Kerouac, Herb Gold, Neal Cassady, and mystery writer Virginia Rath.

Most of the homes here are of modest height, many with spectacular gardens peeking out enticingly from behind little fences. However, along Green Street, you will also see some gleaming white skyscrapers. These were built before 1974, at which time San Francisco imposed a 40-foot height limit on new Russian Hill construction.

There is a potpourri of architectural styles on the hill—Victorians, shingles, bungalows, pueblos, high-rises—all jumbled together, many designed by famous architects such as Willis Polk, Julia Morgan, and Lewis Hobart. In some unimaginable way, this jumble all fits together.

Russian Hill is about views. There's no rope tow up the hill; you climb steps to get to the top, so be prepared to huff and puff. Fortunately, these same steps are also a wonderful place to plop down to rest, catch your breath, and look around.

Russian Hill lies between Taylor and Polk (east to west) and Pacific and Francisco (south to north). However, within this area, there are two separate summits. This walk covers the southern summit, which crests on Vallejo between Jones and Taylor.

Beware, there are no public bathrooms here. Plan in advance.

WALKING TIME

Allow an hour and 15 minutes walking time, plus whatever time you need to rest.

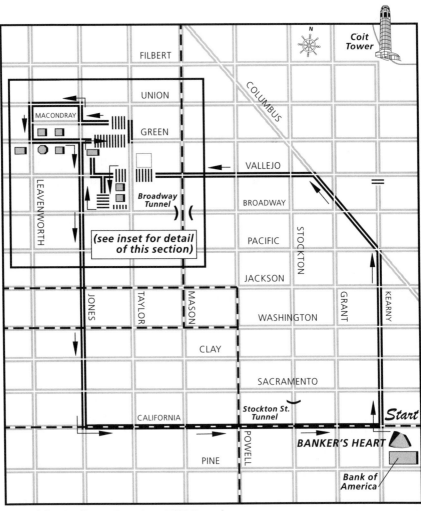

Aerobic Walk to Russian Hill South

GETTING THERE

From the Banker's Heart at Kearny and California, walk north on Kearny until you cross Jackson. Then, turn left (northwest) on Columbus and head to Vallejo. Turn left on Vallejo, and continue until you cross Mason. Take a deep breath and start heading up the Vallejo Steps.

RUSSIAN HILL SOUTH

As you puff up the Vallejo Steps, you are surrounded by greenery and flowers. (On this walk, in public and private gardens, you will see impatiens, ferns, acanthus, pelargonium, hydrangea, geraniums, cotoneaster, ivy, lobelia, cylamen, calla lilies, agapanthus, succulents, and chrysanthemums—some wild, some cultivated.) Turn around often to view the city.

You will come to Ina Coolbrith Park on your right. Russian Hill denizen Ina Coolbrith was the niece of Joseph Smith, founder of the Mormon Church. A friend and confidant of Jack London and Bret

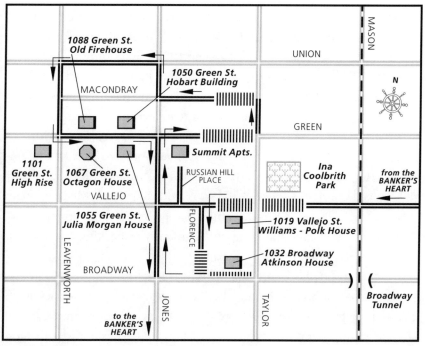

Aerobic Walk to Russian Hill South (inset)

Harte, she held literary soirees and wrote poetry. In 1915 she was named Poet Laureate of California. Her voluminous correspondence with luminaries such as Longfellow, Tennyson, and Dante Gabriel Rossetti was lost forever when her home burned in the great 1906 fire.

Turn right into the park and walk along the path to the little wooden bench at the end. Here you will see a rock with a sign saying "Poet Corner, dedicated by the Ina Coolbrith Circle, 1984." You can sit on the solitary bench and write a poem.

Return to the main path. Cross Taylor and continue hiking up. This part of the stairway was designed by architect Willis Polk and has benefited from neighborhood beautification efforts. As you zigzag back and forth, peek into the beautiful residential gardens.

At the top of the stairway, you enter the historic Vallejo Street Crest District on the summit of Russian Hill. Look directly to your left at the little dark brown shingled duplex at 1019 Vallejo. Designed by Willis Polk in 1892 for Dora Williams, this house sheltered both Mrs. Williams, who lived in one part, and Willis Polk, himself, who lived in the other.

Later on the house was occupied by journalist Rose Wilder. In 1915, she was visited by her mother, Laura Ingalls Wilder of *Little House on the Prairie* fame, who came for the Panama Pacific Exposition. The letters Laura Ingalls Wilder wrote from this quaint house are published in a book, *West from Home*. When you see this rustic dwelling, it is easy to imagine Laura Ingalls Wilder tucked away in a corner, pen in hand.

Stroll around the summit block. Much of the property here was owned by engineer and businessman Horatio P. Livermore and later by his family. Cutting in on the north side of Vallejo is Russian Hill Place, a tiny red-bricked cul-de-sac. Here Willis Polk built four small Mediterranean villas at 1, 3, 5, and 7 Russian Hill Place for Horatio Livermore's son, Norman. Russian Hill Place ends incongruously by backing into the rear of the gigantic Summit Apartments.

Cutting in on the south side of Vallejo is narrow Florence, another treasure trove of homes. Notice the Pueblo Revival stucco houses at 35, 37, and 39 Florence. At 40 Florence is the original Livermore brown shingle house, built in 1865, but much remodeled since then—most notably by Willis Polk in 1891 and a century later by Robert A. M. Stern in 1990.

Walk down the steep Florence Steps to Broadway. To your left is 1032 Broadway, one of the city's oldest houses. Built in 1853, the home was occupied by Kate Atkinson, who conducted literary salons here in the 1890s. "Les Jeunes," a writers' group, met in the Atkinson house to talk about art and life. Across the street at 1051 Broadway is the home of writer Herb Gold, and, at 1067 Broadway, the former home of Ina Donna Coolbrith.

On Broadway, walk west to Jones. Then, turn right on Jones to Vallejo. Between Broadway and Vallejo is a pretty block filled with typical San

Looking east on Green at the Summit Apartments

Francisco bay-windowed homes. On the east side of Jones is an archway and double stairway leading back up to the Crest District summit block. In 1915, the neighborhood, led by Horatio Livermore, created several improvements here, including this archway, the adjacent car ramps, and the concrete retaining wall. These improvements were designed by Willis Polk.

At Green, look north at a perfectly framed view of Alcatraz. Then, look to your right and left to see the great skyscrapers on Green that were erected before height limits. Turn right. The 30-story Summit Apartments (999 Green) high-rise was built in 1965 for Joseph Eichler, who is known for designing much of the middle-class housing in the 'burbs.

Directly east of the Summit Apartments on Green is a rocky hillside, a reminder that despite all of civilization's advances, you are, after all, still perched on a mighty steep and rugged slope.

At the east end of the block, enjoy the views, and then descend the long stairway down to Taylor. Turn left on Taylor, and in the middle of the block you will see a flight of little wooden steps leading up to picturesque Macondray Lane. Dark, romantic, and secluded, Macondray Lane is thought to be the model for Barbary Lane in Armistead Maupin's 1976 serial story *Tales of the City*. Past the wooden stairs, you will walk along stone paths, and then through narrow sidewalks to exit back onto Jones. Turn right on Jones to Union. The sidewalk here is partly steps, partly ordinary sidewalk.

At Union turn left to Leavenworth. This block of Union takes a breather from the hill. You will see more typical San Francisco well-kept, bay-windowed homes. At Union and Leavenworth, turn around slowly to enjoy the spectacular views in every direction. Then turn left (south) to return to Green.

At 1101 Green is another white high-rise—this one a 20-story Art Deco structure with lots of ornamentation. Walk left (east) on Green to see a block with every type of house imaginable. At 1088 Green is the

View of Alcatraz and Angel Island from Union and Jones

old Tudor Revival firehouse, Engine #31, designed by Newton J. Tharp in 1907. In the Fifties, the fire house was purchased and renovated by Louise Davies, who donated it to the National Trust for Historic Preservation.

Across the street is the Feusier Octagon House (1067 Green), which was built in 1859 and enlarged about 20 years later by merchant Louis Feusier, who added the octagonal cupola. A number of octagonal houses were build in San Francisco in response to the book *A Home for All* by Orson S. Fowler, which recommended octagonal houses as promoting good health. And maybe they do!

Nearby, at 1055 Green is an 1866 home set into the middle of a little garden. This house was totally remodeled by Julia Morgan around 1915. You can see beribboned bowls of what looks like fruit molded right into the stucco.

At 1050 Green is a beautiful five-story stucco apartment building designed by Lewis Hobart in 1913. With its stately garden, it looks like a noble building taking its rightful place on top of a noble hill.

Continue to the corner of Green and Jones. You are now ready to return.

But wait. You haven't eaten lunch yet! Well, since Russian Hill is residential, there are no lunch places close by. However, if you want to detour a little, try Hamada's Kebab-Key at 1207 Union (at Hyde). This place has great falafel and other wonderful Middle Eastern dishes too. Warning: this is not a fast food place; so don't come if you're in a rush.

GETTING BACK

You are going to return by strolling along the ridge that connects Russian Hill and Nob Hill. You have already done all the hard work of getting yourself up, so now you can have all the fun. At the corner of Jones and Green, head south on Jones to California. You will see wonderful views as you stride along on top of the city.

Between Sacramento and California, you will see lovely Grace Cathedral from the rear. Turn left on California and walk straight down Nob Hill to return to the Banker's Heart.

Looking at St. Patrick's Church from the Esplanade

The Cable Car Turnaround at Powell & Market

San Francisco Shopping Centre & the Mark Reuben Gallery

Well, you're not going to lose weight on this walk because it's the shortest walk in the book. You're just going across the street. But make sure to look around you when you do because you are at the absolute vortex of downtown San Francisco, with its glamour, its seamy side, its natives, its tourists, and its history.

WALKING TIME

Five minutes each way—if you're slow!

GETTING THERE

At the cable car turnaround at Market and Powell, you will find yourself in the midst of San Francisco's rich street scene. Tourists jostle to climb on the cable cars, street artists and panhandlers hustle, peddlers hawk bracelets, hot dogs, newspapers, and pretzels. Proselytizers urge you to avoid fornication and repent.

Cross to the equally busy south side of Market. Slightly to your right is the entrance to the San Francisco Shopping Centre. But before you go in, walk a little to the left to look at the old Emporium building, now Macy's furniture store, and slated to become a Bloomingdale's.

Until the Emporium closed a couple of years ago, it was the grand old dam of San Francisco department stores, complete with rooftop rides for children every Christmas. Built in 1896, the Emporium survived the 1906 quake and fire, and narrowly escaped being dynamited in the panicky aftermath. When Frank A. Leach, superintendent of the nearby U.S. Mint, protested that all the post-quake blasting in the vicinity was destroying the Mint, dynamiting of the Emporium was called off. Today you can see the original elegant facade, which was fortified against future quakes in 1908.

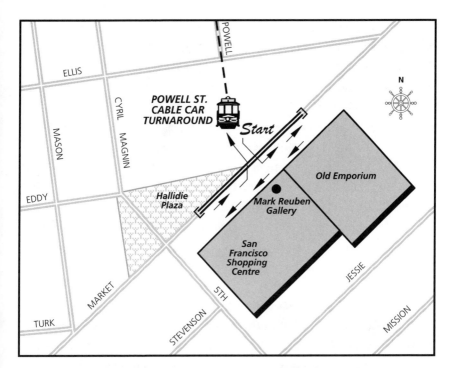

San Francisco Shopping Centre and the Mark Reuben Gallery

Now, walking through Macy's furniture, I find it strange to see coffee tables where I used to buy earrings, and sofas where lipstick should be. But that's progress!

Walk back on Market to the San Francisco Shopping Centre (865 Market). Before the main entrance, you pass a series of the Centre's fanciest shops—Vasari's Impostors, Opals and Gems of Australia, and the Godiva Chocolatier. Continue to the entrance of the Centre and go through the heavy glass doors.

THE SAN FRANCISCO SHOPPING CENTRE

Often called a "vertical" mall, the S.F. Shopping Centre offers nine "shop-till-you-drop" floors (the tenth floor is offices.) When you enter, you will see the Centre's most astonishing feature, a huge curved escalator that slowly winds you upward through the different levels. There are almost 100 shops in this one building—from clothing stores like J. Crew, Victoria's Secret (a lot less sexy than the catalog), Ann Taylor, and

Benetton to the kiddy Gymboree. There are also art galleries, restaurants, health and beauty shops, and even a Sam Goody record store. The Centre is built on land that has been owned by the San Francisco public schools since the 1850s.

As the escalator disgorges you at each level, you must parade past a long line of shops before you can catch the escalator to the next floor. Somehow, I find this completely exhausting and often fall prey to an incapacitating condition my children have dubbed "Shopping Mall Syndrome," but then you can see, I'm not a shopper.

The escalator curves to a stop at Nordstrom, which occupies the top four floors. Here I often recover, helped by an assortment of comfortable chairs and an army of helpful shoe salespeople. Usually, I don't like salespeople fussing over me, but these people really know what they're doing.

THE MARK REUBEN GALLERY

My favorite shop, by far, in the San Francisco Shopping Centre is the Mark Reuben Gallery, located on the street level, to your left when you enter. Often I just come here to browse around and don't bother to go anywhere else.

If you love history, and I do, you'll love the Mark Reuben gallery. This shop sells black-and-white photographs focusing on history, sports, and

Looking up from the escalator at the SF Shopping Centre with Christmas streamers hanging down

entertainment. Do you remember where you were when Kennedy was shot? How about Roosevelt? Do you remember the day World War II ended?

If you do, this will bring it all back. As I looked at the pictures of Churchill and FDR, I remembered VE day (I was very young), with celebratory toilet paper strung in the trees and confetti drifting to the ground. I remember my aunt returning from Times Square and telling us about the people dancing in the streets. If you don't remember because you weren't born, the gallery will give you a flavor of those times.

They've got pictures of Malcolm X and David Ben Gurion, Eleanor Roosevelt and the Kennedy brothers, Amelia Earhart and Pancho Villa. There are lots of pictures of writers and artist too—Mark Twain, Toulouse-Lautrec, Anaïs Nin. The sports collection is also tops. It's easy to lose yourself in old photos of Joe Louis, Stan Musial, and Joe DiMaggio, and forget the hours rolling by.

As you can see I like this place and have even bought a large photo of Mark Twain here, which hangs on my bathroom wall.

Note: There are several other Mark Reuben galleries in the city if you can't get to this one.

GETTING BACK

When you're shopped out, just cross back over Market and you are back at the cable car turnaround.

Sprung from controversy, Yerba Buena Center today spreads over 87 acres of what was once considered "blight." It extends from Market to Harrison and from Second to Fourth and contains the San Francisco Museum of Modern Art, Yerba Buena Gardens, many galleries, Moscone Convention Center, three hotels, and 2,300 residential units, ranging from pricey condos to low-income housing. Yerba Buena Center is still under development with the Mexican and Jewish museums scheduled to move here soon. A huge children's center is being built on top of Moscone Convention South.

The controversy erupted because the blight actually consisted of rooming houses and hotels that housed San Francisco's poor and also of many small businesses including cheap restaurants, pawn shops, and second-hand stores. All this was demolished to build the massive arts, hotel, and convention center.

Residents—some of whom were retired labor activists—and small business owners sued to stop the demolition, and in 1973, in exchange for permission to tear down the area, the San Francisco Redevelopment Agency agreed to provide 2,000 replacement units. However, this housing did not come close to replacing what was lost.

This history added poignant irony to the art exhibit my husband and I saw in Yerba Buena Gardens on its opening day. The exhibit (I think it was called *Circling the Wagons*) consisted of a mute circle of homeless people's carts.

The showpiece of Yerba Buena Center is Yerba Buena Gardens—a swath of green open space in crowded downtown—and that's where this walk takes you. The entire Gardens sits on top of the expanded Moscone Convention Center.

Is Yerba Buena Gardens art or artsy? You will have to decide for yourself.

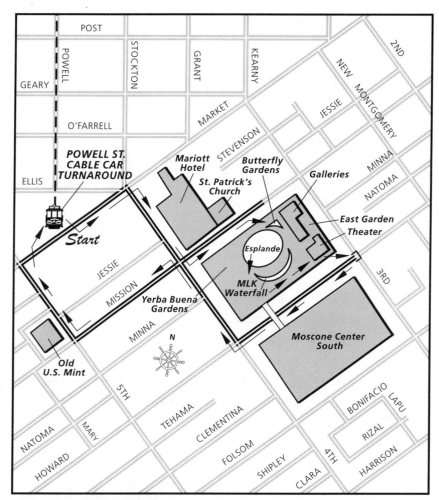

POST

POWELL

STOCKTON

GRANT

KEARNY

2ND

NEW MONTGOMERY

GEARY

JESSIE

O'FARRELL

MARKET

STEVENSON

POWELL ST. CABLE CAR TURNAROUND

ELLIS

Mariott Hotel

Butterfly Gardens

Galleries

MINNA

NATOMA

St. Patrick's Church

Start

East Garden Theater

JESSIE

Esplande

3RD

MISSION

MLK Waterfall

Yerba Buena Gardens

MINNA

N

Moscone Center South

Old U.S. Mint

5TH

TEHAMA

CLEMENTINA

BONIFACIO

LAPU

NATOMA

MARY

FOLSOM

RIZAL

HOWARD

SHIPLEY

CLARA

4TH

HARRISON

Yerba Buena Gardens

WALKING TIME

About 10 minutes getting there, about 15 minutes getting back. Allow at least a half-hour to wander around the Gardens.

GETTING THERE

From the cable car turnaround at Market and Powell, cross Market and walk northeast until you cross Fourth. Turn right, go one block to Mission, and cross. You are at Yerba Buena Gardens, which takes up the entire block. Walk along Mission until you can enter and begin exploring.

YERBA BUENA GARDENS

The most noticeable feature of Yerba Buena Gardens is the Esplanade, a gigantic oval meadow that should receive an award as the "Best Place to Sun Yourself in San Francisco" or perhaps "Best Outdoor Snooze in the Bay Area." It is well-used, as you will see by the numbers of people staking out spots on the grass to eat, sleep, or take in the activities.

The meadow contains an outdoor performance theater, which offers wonderful free noontime events. You can enjoy poetry and prose readings, theater, dance, and concerts of all types—jazz, pop, swing, and classical. One of my favorite theater groups, the San Francisco Mime Troop performs here. (You can pick up a schedule listing dates and times of events.) From the center of the meadow, you have a perfect view of modest Saint Patrick's Church and the ostentatious Marriott Hotel juxtaposed across Mission Street.

The second "most notable feature" is the Martin Luther King memorial and waterfall south of the meadow. You walk behind the 50-foot-wide, 20-foot-high granite waterfall to view the memorial, which consists of glass panels inscribed with Dr. King's quotations. The first reads "No we are not satisfied, and we will not be satisfied until justice rolls down like water and righteousness like a mighty stream." And, in fact, the waterfall does roar mightily. It's wet and slippery behind, so be careful as you walk.

Another enjoyable spot is the Butterfly Gardens at the northeast end of the meadow. This garden's beautiful plantings provide habitat for several

The Esplanade at Yerba Buena Gardens

Martin Luther King, Jr. Memorial Waterfall

special of local butterflies. None were in evidence, the day I was there, but maybe the butterflies hadn't read the brochure. There's also an East Garden, across from the San Francisco Museum of Modern Art, which contains a cascading fountain with a little terrace that lets you sit practically in the water. In the same area is John Roloff's sculpture *Deep Gradient/Suspect Terrain*, the 18-foot-high hull of a green glass ship.

On the opposite side of the meadow is a tribute to California's Ohlone Indians created in the form of a circle of rock benches and a small crescent pool. Behind this is a wooden wall patterned with Ohlone basket designs. The area is designed for intimate performances in the oral tradition—storytelling or poetry reading. The monument, *Oché Wat Té Ou/Reflection*, was created by Native American artists Jaune Quick-to-See Smith and James Luna.

If you want to go indoors and spend money, you can do that too. There's the Center for the Arts Galleries and Forum, which features work by local artists. It contains three galleries, a media room for showing videos, and some exhibition space. There's also a gift shop and café. Admission to the galleries is free only from 6 to 8 P.M. the first Thursday of the month.

There's also the Center for the Arts Theater, which hosts theater and dance events with a focus on non-profit and local groups.

At the west side of the King memorial/waterfall, walk up the steps to the Garden's upper level. Here you can more readily sense that you are on top of the Convention Center. At this level are some lunch cafés and many more pleasant places to sit. In fact, you can sit right at the top of the rushing waterfall and take in the action in the meadow below. The sandwich I bought at Pasqua's here cost a dollar more than the same sandwich at Pasqua's at the Bank of America building, so you might want to bring your lunch from elsewhere.

On the way to the upper level, you will see Terry Allen's *Shaking Man*, a life-size bronze sculpture of a business man with a few extra hands and feet. He is offering his hands to shake, and he seems to be shaking spiritually as well.

GETTING BACK WITH A LOOK AT THE OLD U.S. MINT

You are going to exit the gardens at Howard Street, the south end. If you want to see the Gardens sitting on top of the Convention Center, take the steps down to Howard at the east end of the upper level. Then, cross Howard at Third. Walk back along Howard to Fourth and look across the street to see Yerba Buena Gardens sitting right on top of Moscone Convention Center North.

If you don't care about this experience, take the pedestrian overpass on the west end of the upper level, which walks you right over Howard Street. You descend at the corner of Howard and Fourth.

In either case, when you get to Howard and Fourth, walk north a block to Mission and then turn left to Fifth and Mission for a quick look at the Old U.S. Mint on the northwest corner.

Sadly, the Mint Museum has been closed since 1994, so you can't go in, but it's still worth looking at because of the rich part this building played in San Francisco's history. The original mint was located on 608 Commercial Street (see "Walk 11"), but operations were moved to this massive granite building in 1874 to handle the wealth from the Comstock Lode silver strike. The Mint remained at this location until the 1930s, when it moved to 155 Hermann Street. In 1973, the mint at Fifth and Mission opened as a museum.

During the great quake and fire, the Mint and its gold were saved from destruction by devoted employees who risked their lives in their endeavors. Since the fire destroyed all the city's banks—including many depositor records and bank notes—the Mint served as the city's financial institution after the quake, distributing relief funds to the population, and letting customers from disabled banks make withdrawals and start rebuilding.

In his 1917 memoir *Recollections of a Newspaperman*, Frank Leach, journalist and superintendent of the Mint describes the events. Making his way from his Oakland home to San Francisco the morning of the quake, he saw both sides of Market Street in flames. Fighting his way past soldiers, he finally reached the Mint, where with 50 other employees and 10 soldiers from Fort Miley, he worked to save the building. Leach writes:

> The men in relays dashed into the rooms to play water on the flames; they met a fierce heat; though scorched was their flesh, each relay would remain in these places, which were veritable furnaces, as long as they could hold their breaths, then come out to be relieved by another crew of willing fighters.[13]

After the fire, Superintendent Leach installed pipes from the Mint's artesian well to provide the homeless tenting in the surrounding area with fresh water. Thus, the area around the Mint became a little refugee village.

When you look at the boarded-up Mint today, it's hard to guess at its exciting past.

Continue north on Fifth to return to Hallidie Plaza.

---

[13] Frank A. Leach. *Recollections of a Newspaperman* (San Francisco: Samuel Levinson, 1917), p.326.

San Francisco Museum of Modern Art

Growing up in New York, where I spent weekends wandering around the Metropolitan Museum of Art, the Guggenheim, and the Museum of Modern Art,[14] I had a snotty attitude toward San Francisco museums when I first came here in 1965.

"Museums?" I used to sneer, "What museums?"

Always remembering New York, where Rembrandts at the Metropolitan cluster on the walls like, well, like Rembrandts at the Metropolitan, I simply could not get excited by the modest offerings of the M.H. de Young in Golden Gate Park or the San Francisco Museum of Art at its old digs in the War Memorial Veterans Building.

But one day I accepted the fact that I wasn't in New York and started actually enjoying the museums here.

WALKING TIME

About 25 minutes round trip, not counting time spent in the Museum.

GETTING THERE

From the cable car turnaround at Market and Powell, walk northeast on Market Street, toward the Ferry Building. Notice how pretty the Ferry Building looks at the end of the street. Also, notice the Flood Building (870 Market). Built in 1904 by James L. Flood in memory of his father, silver baron James C. Flood, this flatiron building was once San Francisco's biggest building. As you walk along, you will encounter some creative street artists and many panhandlers.

---

[14] Note that it's not called the *New York* Museum of Modern Art. New Yorkers have so much hubris that they assume theirs is the only one that counts.

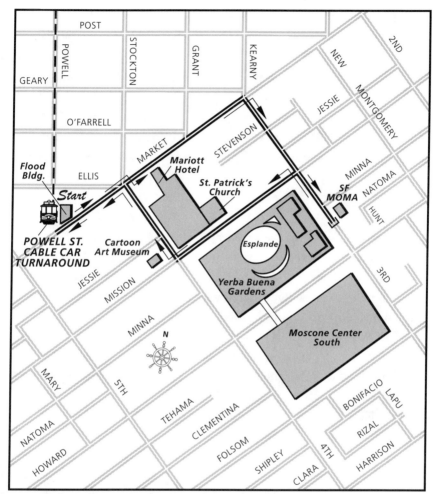

San Francisco Museum of Modern Art

The corner of Market, Ellis, and Stockton was, until very recently, the place to get an inexpensive slice of real New York pizza at Escape from New York. The sign in the window claimed, "All the taste. Half the attitude." (The pizzeria recently closed and is reopening at 333 Bush Street in the fall of 1998.)

When I first came to San Francisco, I kept hunting for a slice of pizza that tasted like "real" pizza, *i.e.*, the way it tasted in New York. Therefore, I was at Escape From New York the day it opened.

"This is a test," I said to the man behind the counter. "I'm from New York. In fact from the Bronx, and I know what real New York pizza tastes like."

"Lady, I c'n take da presha," he answered, without looking up.

Cross Market at Stockton and continue past the Marriott Hotel. During the walk, you will view this unusual structure (some call it "the juke box") from all four sides. Cross Third Street and turn right. Past Mission, you will come to the San Francisco Museum of Modern Art at 131 Third.

SFMOMA

It's modern all right. Designed by Swiss architect Mario Botta, this ultra avant-garde structure is distinguished by a gigantic cylindrical black-and-white striped skylight that emerges from the roof. This skylight provides so much light that as you walk from floor to floor, you keep thinking you're outside when you're actually inside.

SFMOMA moved to its present location in January of 1995. It is open from 11 A.M. to 6 P.M. every day but Wednesdays. On Thursdays, it stays open until 9 P.M. Adult admission is $8, with the first Tuesday of each month free.

The day I was there—an ordinary, non-free Thursday—the Museum was jammed. In fact the little museum restaurant, Caffè Museo, was so crowded, I had to retreat to the donut shop down the street to get a cup of coffee.

The Museum has five floors, the ground floor taken up by the Museum Store, the restaurant, and a very New Yorkish coat-check room. The permanent collection on the second floor has a lot to offer. I particularly enjoyed works by Georges Rouault, Alberto Giacometti, and Georgia O'Keefe. Other floors house the Museum's exciting photography collection and also special exhibits, which, on the day I was there, included a fabulous retrospective by sculptor Robert Arneson. Arneson is the artist who created the statue of assassinated Mayor George Moscone, a statue so controversial that it had to be removed from the Moscone Center and placed in—where else?—SFMOMA.

©SFMOMA/Richard Barnes 1994

SFMOMA

GETTING BACK—WITH DETOUR TO
THE CARTOON ART MUSEUM

Return to Mission and turn left. You will see Yerba Buena Gardens (subject of "Walk 26") on your left and pretty Saint Patrick's church (756 Mission) across the street. Remember to look up at the Marriott.

The proximity of the vast Yerba Buena Gardens to the equally vast numbers of homeless in the area always makes me wonder if some of these homeless didn't used to live in the single-room-occupancy hotels (or "furnished rooms" as we New Yorkers once called them) that were torn down to create the Gardens. In the Seventies, some people protested, "But where will the occupants go?" Now, it's all too obvious many didn't go anywhere. Only their rooms went.

At Fourth, cross Mission and, if you want to see a different type of art, continue to the Cartoon Art Museum on the second floor of 814 Mission. Housed in the 1920s *San Francisco Bulletin* building and

©SFMOMA/Richard Barnes 1994

The interior of SFMOMA

squashed up against Catholic Charities, this Museum is a total contrast
from trendy SFMOMA and the Yerba Buena Gardens. You can even see
ink splotches from the newspaper days on the Museum floor. (The Bay
Area Rapid Transit District also had offices here in the mid-to-late
Sixties.)

The Cartoon Art Museum is definitely not yuppie. Trust me on this.
The elevators are so dinky, you will pray as you rise.

Inside, it's wonderful—dark, old and woody. Founded in 1984 by a
group of cartoon devotees, the Museum is open Wednesday through
Friday 11 A.M. to 5 P.M., Saturday 10 A.M. to 5 P.M., and Sunday 1 P.M. to
5 P.M. Adult admission is $4, with the first Wednesday of the month as
free day—or rather, pay-what-you-can-day.

The collection contains cartoons from William Hogarth (1730s) to
Cathy Guisewite. The Museum also sponsors about eight exhibitions a
year, and an artists-in-residence program that has offered lectures and
round-table discussions by eminent cartoonists such as Charles Schulz
and Art Spiegelman.

The bookstore sells, among other wonderful things, original editorial art. For about $50, you can buy the originals of some of the editorial cartoons you see in the newspapers.

When you exit the Museum, return to Fourth Street, and turn left toward Market. If you have time, you can actually enter the Marriott (You've already shot most of the afternoon; why not just take the rest of the day off!) and take a High Rise elevator to the View Lounge at the 39th floor. The views are extraordinary, but, as this lounge is actually a place where they sell food and drink, I wouldn't overstay my welcome.

If you don't have time for the Marriott, you can browse in the window of Cole Fox Hardware on the corner of Fourth and Jessie (70 4th Street). This is the only hardware store in the area, and it's very well stocked.

On Fourth continue to Market and then turn left to return to the cable car turnaround.

The Theater District

In San Francisco *the* theater district has traditionally referred to the area around Geary Street just west of Union Square. This neighborhood is also overflowing with tourist shops, art galleries, shoe-shine stands, eateries, and mammoth luxury hotels. And, although you probably won't notice them because they work hard at being inconspicuous, the city's most exclusive private clubs are also ensconced here. The whole district has an upbeat feel and is far less tawdry than Times Square, its New York counterpart.

San Francisco theater is a mix of transported Broadway shows, ensembles, repertory, experimental, ethnic, and gay/lesbian theater, and in September the "anything goes" Fringe Festival. On the Stockton side of Union Square, where Maiden Lane ends, is a half-price ticket booth, where you can often get discount tickets for same-day performances (and full-price tickets for future shows). The booth is open Monday–Thursday.

Of course there are other districts in San Francisco that offer theater—the Mission, the Castro, Market Street, Japantown, and the Tenderloin, but they're not *the* theater district.

WALKING TIME

Half an hour, not counting riding the elevator at the Westin St. Francis or exploring inside the theaters or hotel lobbies.

GETTING THERE

From the cable car turnaround at Market and Powell, follow the cable car tracks north to O'Farrell. Turn left. This block is solid hotels, some quite sumptuous. At Mason, turn right. Behind you, the gigantic and posh San Francisco Hilton Towers fills the *entire* block from Mason to Taylor and from O'Farrell to Ellis.

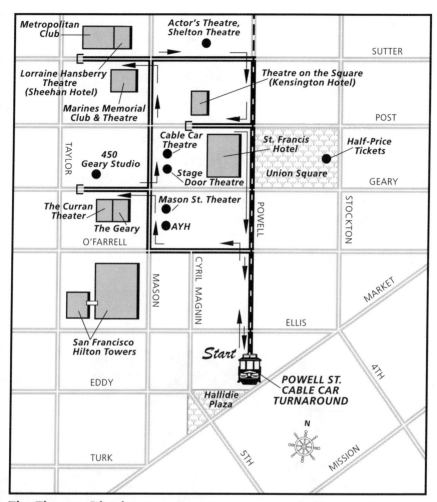

The Theater District

For those requiring more humble accommodation, the American Youth Hostel (AYH) is also here at 312 Mason. Next door, at 308 Mason, is the AYH Travel Center, which used to be full of wonderful products like enchanted towels that dried you in the wilderness without getting wet themselves, and clothespins that safely dangled your clothes over rocky crevasses. Now, however, the Travel Center mainly sells books and the sleep sheets required for Hostel stayovers.

Right past the Youth Hostel, and just as modest, is the little Mason Street Theater (340 Mason) marking your entrance into the theater district. Turn left at Geary and you will come upon two of San Francisco's most glamorous theaters—the Curran and the Geary.

THE THEATERS

The elegant Geary Theater (415 Geary) is home to the American Conservatory Theater (ACT), a premier repertory company that has launched stars such as Danny Glover, Annette Bening, Denzel Washington, and Winona Ryder. ACT's respected actor training program serves 1,400 students a year.

Built in 1909, the Geary was damaged in the Loma Prieta quake and closed for seven years for renovation, but it's back in business now. Notice the terra cotta panels with their blue backgrounds and golden garlands and fruits.

Photo by Marco Lorenzetti. ©Korab Hedrich Blessing

The interior of the Geary Theater

Right next door is the equally elegant Curran (445 Geary), built in 1922. This is the place to see Broadway shows in San Francisco. At the time of this writing, the Curran was showing *Phantom of the Opera*.

Across Geary, tucked in among the kosher restaurant, the pizza joint, and the Paisley Hotel is the 450 Geary Studio Theatre, an intimate playhouse that presents innovative solo performers and small ensembles. The Artfull Circle Theatre group, a drag acting company has performed its yearly musical *Christmas with the Crawfords* here.

Now return to Mason and continue north. The block between Geary and Post is crowded with galleries, more giant hotels, and also more theaters. You will pass the Stage Door Theatre—currently closed—with the cozy Cable Car Theatre right next door (430 Mason). On this block is also the Native Sons Building (414 Mason) and on the corner, the First Congregational Church and the giant Donatello Hotel. You are now on the lower slopes of Nob Hill and heading uphill.

Cross Post and pass the even larger Pan Pacific Hotel, which offers visitors high-tech conference facilities. The hotel land is owned by the private Olympic Club, around the corner at 524 Post. At Sutter, turn left into another cluster of theaters. Inside of the Marines Memorial Club building (609 Sutter), the Marines Memorial Theatre presents local, touring, and Broadway shows. The Club itself is a living memorial to U.S. Marines who were killed, lost, or died in military service. You can walk inside and browse commemorative exhibits, photos, and books. During World War II, the building was a women's club that housed WACS, WAVES, Women Marines, and SPARS. The theater is on the second floor.

Across the street in the Sheehan Hotel (620 Sutter) is the Lorraine Hansberry Theatre, featuring plays by black writers and providing opportunities for black actors, designers, directors, writers, and technicians.

The large, yet unobtrusive, big brick building to the left of the Sheehan Hotel is the Metropolitan Club (640 Sutter), one of the exclusive, San Francisco private women's clubs.

Now head east on Sutter toward Union Square. Sutter from Mason to Powell is filled with fascinating stores and galleries. Look at the old and rare books and prints in the Bookstall (570 Sutter) and at the doll houses and miniatures in the Treasure House (563 Sutter).

There are two tiny theaters at 533 Sutter. On the second floor is the Actors Theatre. This is a collective where the actors and directors produce experimental plays, working toward a shared artistic vision rather than toward individual recognition. On the first floor is the Shelton Theatre, home of the Jean Shelton Acting Lab.

Continue to Powell and turn right to Post. Then turn right again to the Theatre on the Square, which offers new works and touring productions of all kinds—musicals, comedies, and dramas. The theater is actually inside of the Kensington Park Hotel (450 Post), which was once the Elks Club. Look inside at the lobby, filled with old furniture and woodwork. Again, the theater is on the second floor.

GETTING BACK WITH DETOUR INTO THE WESTIN ST. FRANCIS

To return, walk back to Powell and head south. At 335 Powell is the opulent and legendary Hotel St. Francis—now called the "Westin St. Francis." Built by the Crockers in 1904, the hotel survived the '06 quake but succumbed to its fiery aftermath. The St. Francis was quickly rebuilt, and in 1972, William Periera Associates, the designers of the Transamerica Pyramid, added a modern tower behind the original structure. The new part features external elevators, which you can ride to the 32nd floor.

The hotel is "legendary" not just for its luxuriousness, but because it was the center of the Hollywood/San Francisco Fatty Arbuckle scandal of 1921. Arbuckle, a silent film star and comedian was partying here when a guest named Virginia Rappe became ill. He put her to bed in one of his rooms and soon returned to Hollywood. Several days later Rappe died in a clinic, and Arbuckle was charged with murder and rape. Although Arbuckle was found innocent in court, his career was ruined, and he died young of a heart attack.

Walk through the lobby to experience the sumptuous furnishings, the elegant old carpets, the posh shops, and the sense of a time now past. When you get to the gold revolving doors, turn right and follow the signs to the outdoor elevators.

To see a gorgeous view of the city, take an elevator up to the 32nd floor. At first you can't see anything because the elevator is hidden behind the original St. Francis building, but it emerges quickly to staggering views of the city and the Bay. You can look straight down on Union Square. Actually, looking straight down is somewhat scary, but it's definitely worth the experience.

After you leave the Hotel St. Francis, continue down Powell to return to the cable car turnaround.

Holiday Windows

It takes a little work to get the holiday feel in a town like San Francisco. It takes pretending that thick December rain is crisply falling snow and that foghorns are really sleigh bells. To get in the mood, it helps to walk through the Union Square area to see the windows decked in Christmas finery, the Salvation Army bell ringers, and the street artists outdoing each other to attract your generosity.

Warning: New stores open and landmarks close. When you take this walk, you may see very different stores and displays from the ones I describe.

WALKING TIME

About 40 minutes if you stay *outside* the stores.

GETTING THERE

From the cable car turnaround at Market and Powell, walk north on Powell to O'Farrell. Cross. Then, turn right.

THE WINDOWS

You will be walking by a block-long spread of Macy's Christmas windows. Seated outside are shoppers eating lunch at little tables and listening to holiday music. Although the display varies from year to year, you can usually count on storybook characters and animals—reindeer, elephants, camels, zebras, and bunnies. Turn left at Stockton to view more Macy's windows.

At the time of this writing, the Geary side of Macy's was undergoing renovation, so there wasn't much window dressing, but this situation is temporary. To get more holiday feel, go up to Macy's seventh floor to see Santa and dazzling Christmas trees laden with ornaments. (The ornaments are for sale, but Santa is not!)

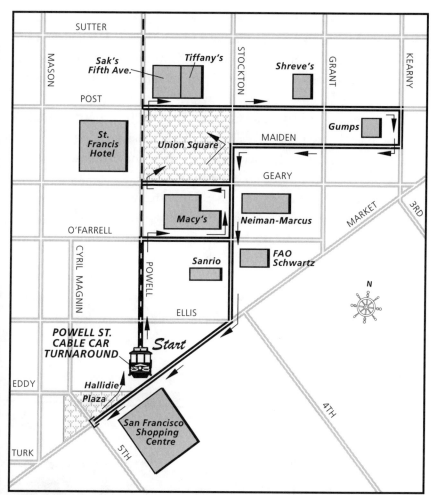

Holiday Windows

Actually Macy's best holiday spread is not at Christmas-time, but at Easter-time, when the store hosts a world-renowned flower show that draws flower-lovers like bears to honey. Comprising hundreds of species and literally millions of blossoms, the flowers grace both the windows and the store's interior. Docents lead eager aficionados through the lavish extravaganza of azaleas and rhododendrons. It's also fun to wander through the blooms on your own and inundate your senses with the colors and scents.

Cross into Union Square to enjoy both the giant Christmas tree and the Chanukah menorah, one candle of which is lit at dusk for the eight nights of Chanukah. At Union Square at Christmas-time, you may find an assortment of bell ringers, musical performances, and police on horseback.

Union Square got its name from the pro-Union orations and rallies that were held here right before the Civil War. Today the Square is best known not as a center for fiery oratory, but as the centerpiece of San Francisco's shopping, hotel, and theater district. Encircled by the glamorous Westin St. Francis, Macy's, Saks Fifth Avenue, Tiffany's, and Gucci, the actual Square itself hosts the same urban problems that plague most other downtown areas—homelessness and panhandling.

Cross the Post at Powell to look into the windows of Saks Fifth Avenue (364 Post) and Tiffany's (350 Post). Saks' window display twirls and twists with holiday glamour; Tiffany's windows are more modest, their display created by the developmentally disabled for an annual bazaar.

The holiday season at Union Square

Continue east on Post and cross Stockton. You will pass Armani, Laura Ashley, Alfred Dunhill, Ann Taylor, and other shops, all arrayed in holiday finery. At the corner of Post and Grant, you will come to Shreve's, a San Francisco jewelry store dating from 1852. It's distinguished, elegant, and very expensive.

Continue on Post to Gump's (135 Post). Opened in 1861, Gump's is a store that defies categorization. It calls itself a department store, but you wouldn't come here for a pair of jeans or a backpack. You might come for a statue, fine china and crystal, or a piece of imported furniture. Gump's is a major importer of Asian arts.

The windows are small but exquisitely decorated. They attract a crowd, but not as big a crowd as Gump's Christmas windows did in their previous location at 350 Post, when they were filled with tumbling kittens and puppies being offered for adoption by the SPCA. On the fourth floor is Gump's holiday store, where you can buy a Christmas ornament for $100.

Pass Gump's and turn right on Kearny. Turn right again on Maiden Lane and follow it all the way back to Stockton (see "Walk 14" for more on Maiden Lane.) Here you will find small boutiques and eateries that provide a breather from the crowded holiday streets.

At Stockton turn left and cross Geary. On the corner is Neiman-Marcus (150 Stockton). The windows are luxuriously wonderful, but more wonderful is the interior, where you can gaze upward at the tree-filled rotunda which rises four stories to a skylit dome. This is the famous City of Paris rotunda, which was left untouched when the Neiman-Marcus store was built on the site of the old City of Paris in 1983.

Past Neiman-Marcus at Stockton and O'Farrell is FAO Schwartz (48 Stockton), where a gentleman in top hat (really a starving college student on winter break) beckons you inside. The interior is a kids' paradise from the stuffed bear section to the Barbie Boutique where you can view hundreds of Barbie's shoes freely floating in the Barbie Bubbler. (Over one billion Barbie shoes have been sold.)

Across Stockton is another kids' paradise—the Sanrio store of Hello Kitty fame (39 Stockton). Inside is a glittery world of rainbows and bridges leading to magic kingdoms.

Continue on Stockton to Market, cross and turn right to San Francisco's holiday *pièce de résistance*—Nordstrom's windows. Here you will see a no-expense-spared production that whirls you into a fairy-tale world of pirouetting princes and enchanted swans. The windows gleam with the opulence and extravagance of an era before cost-cutting and "bottom-line" considerations. Don't miss them.

GETTING BACK

Continue to Fifth Street. Then cross Market to return to the cable car turnaround.

Civic Center— UN Plaza & the Library

This is the first of two walks that cover the Civic Center area. I broke the territory into two walks because, if you take a leisurely look around the library, you're probably not going to have enough time to explore the Civic Center buildings thoroughly. However, if you *have* the time, you can "do" all of Civic Center in one fell swoop.

One thing I find difficult to explain to my kids is that when I came to San Francisco in 1965, there were no homeless people on Market Street. In fact, you could walk from the Ferry Building to Civic Center and not see one panhandler, not see one soiled sleeping bag with its pathetic occupant stretched against a doorway. Howard Street, "yes," other south of Market streets, "yes," but not on Market itself. Today, however, as you walk along Market and explore UN Plaza and the Civic Center area, the homeless are actually the dominant feature. In some ways this walk can't help but be a tour of San Francisco's homeless population.

Although Market Street gets seamy, it's well-populated and not dangerous—at least not during daylight hours. Take this walk on Wednesday, so you can enjoy the wonderful farmers' market at UN Plaza.

WALKING TIME

About half an hour not counting time spent browsing in the library.

GETTING THERE

From the cable car turnaround at Market and Powell, walk southwest on Market. You pass a wonderful melange of tourists, street people, vendors offering assorted goods on rickety card tables, and my favorite—the chess players slumped deep in concentration while crowds of onlookers discuss strategy.

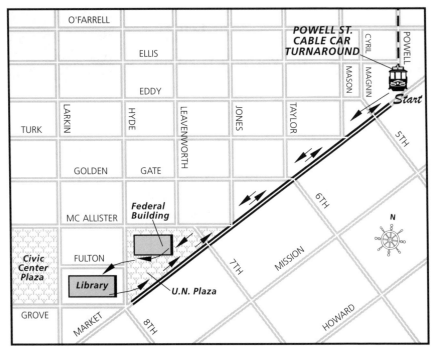

Civic Center - U.N. Plaza and the Library

As you continue, the crowds thin—just a bit. Market Street, at this point, is a jumble of little stores—smoke shops, billiards halls, x-rated dives, delis, discount camera stores, passport photo shops, shoe repair shacks, locksmiths, photo shops, discount luggage stores, hamburger joints, and check cashing services. Continue past Seventh Street North and you will see UN Plaza on your right.

UN PLAZA AND THE FARMERS' MARKET

With its recessed spurting fountain at one end and its imposing statue of Simon Bolivar at the other, the UN Plaza commemorates the signing of the United Nations charter in June of 1945. Austere columns, engraved with the names of UN member nations, line the walkway. The actual signing took place at the Veterans Auditorium (today called Herbst Theatre) in the War Memorial Veterans Building, where, under the eye of Temporary Secretary-General Alger Hiss, representatives of 51 nations met and signed the charter.

UN Plaza with City Hall in the background

Today the homeless have pretty much claimed UN Plaza. However, on Wednesday and Sundays, a huge farmers' market fills the area. Overflowing fruit and vegetable stands provide a contrast to the all-too-evident surrounding destitution.

This farmers' market seems much more "down to earth" than the upscale Tuesday market at the Ferry Building. No chips and dips at UN Plaza. Instead, you see beets, radishes, carrots, eggplants, tomatoes, iced fish, and occasionally some live chickens pecking at their crates. Many of the shoppers and vendors are Asian, so there is lots of bok choy and bitter melon. The sheer quantity of fruits and vegetables—ever changing with the seasons—creates an appealing cornucopia.

LIBRARY

When you're through wandering around the farmers' market and sampling the wares, walk past the statue of Simon Bolivar and continue to the Fulton Street entrance of the new San Francisco Main Library, which has entrances on Grove, Fulton, and Larkin (the actual address is 100 Larkin). You will enter on the library's second floor.

Do I love new Main? I'm getting used to it.

The skylighted atrium of the New Main

My idea of a perfect library is an endlessly long shelf of books numbered in strict Dewey Decimal from 000 to 999. You look up the book you
want in the catalog (card or on-line), write down the number, and then
walk along the shelf until you find your book. If there's something wrong
with this system, I've never figured out what it is.

The new library isn't like this.

New Main opened in its new location on April 18, 1996, ninety years
to the day and on the identical spot where, San Francisco's library collapsed during the Great Quake. It replaces the Main Library, which was
built in 1917, and stands just on the other side of Fulton Street. (Old
Main is now slated to become the Asian Museum.)[15]

In new Main, over 300 computer terminals replace the old card catalog. The building itself is a large, skylighted, open structure, with a grand
staircase leading up from the Grove Street entrance. Many community

---

[15] On the Fulton/Larkin corner of the library is the kinetic sculpture *Double L. Excentric Gyratory* by
George Rickey. An accompanying plaque states that the sculpture is a gift from immigrant Carl
Djerassi (developer of the birth control pill) to his adopted city. If you take "Walk 6," you will see
another Rickey sculpture in Sydney G. Walton Square.

groups have areas here: There's a Teen Center, a Chinese Center, a Filipino American Center, an African American Center, an International Center, a Children's Creative Center, and so on. This is no musty darkened, quiet library of yore.

Unfortunately, with so many centers, I sometimes have trouble finding my book and this makes me grumpy. Looking up a book on one of the many terminals is not the problem; finding the actual book is. At first, I wandered around mumbling "Where are the stacks? Where are the stacks?" And, after some hunting, I did find Main's general collection (aka the stacks) on the third floor. Then I felt a little more at home.

But maybe I'm just old and cranky. My daughter takes books out of Main all the time, and she never has any trouble.

GETTING BACK

Simply return down Market to the cable car turnaround. There's no simpler way of getting back.

Civic Center Again—
City Hall & the Arts

By day, Civic Center is the seat of San Francisco's government. The mayor, the Board of Supervisors, various commissioners—they all meet here. On weekends and at night, Civic Center transforms into an arts center filled with opera, symphony, dance, and lectures.

As part of the City Beautiful movement, Chicago Architect Daniel Burnham, creator of Chicago's Columbian Exposition Fair of 1893, came to San Francisco in 1904 to design a Civic Center that would transform San Francisco into a glamorous Paris. Surrounding City Hall would be palatial symphony and opera houses. Wide boulevards would radiate out from the city's Civic Center.

During the '06 quake, the existing City Hall conveniently tumbled down, allowing planners to start with a clean slate. Then, in 1911, Mayor "Sunny Jim" Rolph announced a competition with a first prize of $25,000 for a design of a new City Hall. To expedite matters, San Franciscans approved an eight million dollar bond issue in 1912 to finance the civic complex.

The competition winners were the firm of Bakewell and Brown, and they broke ground in April of 1913. The new City Hall was completed and dedicated on December 29, 1915. Other buildings followed—the old Main Library (a block north of new Main), the Veterans Memorial Building, and in 1932, the War Memorial Opera House.

Without doubt, the centerpiece of Civic Center is City Hall. The dome is modeled after St. Peter's Basilica in Rome. The building is huge, measuring 400 by 300 feet. With its Doric columns and gilt-trimmed balconies, City Hall is the epitome of both grandeur and elegance.

Alas, today the grandeur of City Hall only heightens the ironic contrast with the scene of unmitigated human misery and total destitution that surrounds it—the homeless shuffling along Civic Center's paths, poking through trash cans, or stretched asleep on their benches.

WALKING TIME

An hour and forty-five minutes.

GETTING THERE

As you did for "Walk 30," stroll southwest on Market from the cable car turnaround at Market and Powell until you pass Seventh Street North. Then, turn right into UN Plaza. Ahead of you, you will see imposing City Hall.

Walk though UN Plaza and continue on Fulton. The New Main Library will be on your left. In front of you is controversial Pioneer Monument.

PIONEER MONUMENT, CIVIC CENTER PLAZA, AND CITY HALL

Financed by James Lick and sculpted by Frank Happersberger, the Pioneer Monument was erected in 1894 at the corner of Grove, Hyde, and Market streets, near the site of the old City Hall. The monument was recently moved to its present location, precipitating a gigantic controversy.

The monument consists of groups of life-sized cast-iron figures depicting the life of California's early settlers. One of the groupings shows a Native American kneeling submissively before a Franciscan friar and a Spanish California vaquero. (Local winos frequently tuck a beer bottle into the vaquero's upraised hand.) During the construction of the new Main Library, a huge dispute erupted about the plaque that would accompany this grouping. Native Americans understandably found the statues insulting, so a plaque was proposed that included this text: "...in 1834, the missionaries left behind about 56,000 converts—and 150,000 dead. Half of the original Native American population had perished during this time from disease, armed attacks, and mistreatment."

Native Americans still objected because they said it understated the number of dead. The SF Catholic Archdiocese and Consul General of

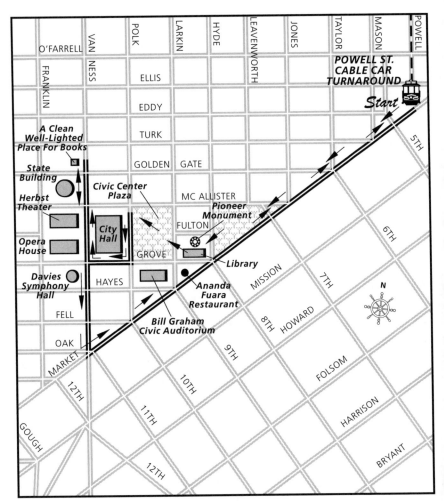

Civic Center Again - City Hall and the Arts

Spain (home of the founding missionaries), also objected because they felt they were being blamed for the deaths. Finally, a plaque was approved that was at least minimally acceptable to all.

The day I was there, someone had set grapes on top of this plaque for the homeless who were sleeping in the Monument.

After viewing the Monument, cross Larkin into the heart of Civic Center Plaza.

This large grassy area is actually the top of—you guessed it—a parking garage. A stately double column of trees promenades you to City Hall. To the right, the Pavilion of American Flags once flew the 18 American flags (from pre-Betsy Ross to our current flag). However, the Pavilion was flagless when I was last there, and it looked like an empty swimming pool. The Plaza's large grassy lawns and flower beds, containing agapanthus, lobelia, iris, lavender, and geraniums, provide additional bedrooms for the homeless. At the northeast corner a brave, fenced-in totlot warns "No adults admitted unless accompanied by children." During the week, this totlot is filled with happily oblivious tots.

Just south of Civic Center Plaza is the Bill Graham Civic Auditorium, host to various concerts and events, And to the west, directly in front of you, is majestic City Hall.

San Francisco's City Hall is the crown jewel of San Francisco. Its sandstone and marble dome is actually higher than the US Capitol in Washington, and it is considered one of the finest examples of classical architecture in the United States. Because of its size, Beaux Art design, and striking architecture, City Hall has lent itself to hosting many visiting dignitaries and formal state events. President Harding's funeral was held here in 1923. On an even more somber note, on November 28,

The controversial Pioneer Monument

1978, City Hall was the site of the assassination of Mayor George Moscone and supervisor Harvey Milk by ex-supervisor Dan White.

City Hall was seriously damaged in the Loma Prieta quake in 1989 and it is currently closed for extensive seismic retrofit and earthquake damage repair. So, right now, you can't go in. I admit I have not been inside, but I plan to go the minute City Hall reopens, which may not be until the 21st century. I have heard that the great interior rotunda is majestic, as is the stairway that leads up to what once was the mayor's office.

You should walk entirely around this building to view its elegance and rich detail from every angle.

THE ARTS

When you are through viewing City Hall, walk west on McAllister to Van Ness Avenue. Cross Van Ness and McAllister to view the big round State Building with its gigantic seal. Stretching south from here is an imposing lineup of San Francisco's arts.

Note: If you want to take a break from buildings and monuments, continue north a little way to A Clean Well Lighted Place for Books, an independent bookstore at 601 Van Ness Avenue. Here, you can rest and recharge your batteries while browsing through the eclectic selection—computer books, small press titles, erotica, business books, best sellers, and opera books. The store also has a great children's section.

Just south of McAllister at 401 Van Ness is Herbst Theatre in the Veterans Building. (The Veterans Building also housed the San Francisco Museum of Modern Art until it moved to its current posh digs on Third Street.)

Built in the 1930s and renovated in 1978, Herbst Theater is a complete, yet intimate, theater with orchestra, boxes, dress circle, and balcony, which hosts dance and music events such as the Women's Philharmonic. The theater seats 928 and includes a full-service bar. Today, its most popular happening is the City Arts and Lectures series, which brings cultural luminaries to San Francisco. Notables have Ursula Hegi, Frank McCourt, Amos Oz, and Grace Paley.

On the third and fourth floors of the Veterans Building, you can view artwork by local artists.

Directly south, past the blue and gold gates, is the War Memorial Opera House at 301 Van Ness. The luxurious Opera House opened on October 15, 1932, with a performance of Puccini's *Tosca*. Designed by Arthur Brown, Jr. (the same Brown who designed City Hall), the Opera House seats 3,525 and is the home of both the opera and the ballet. America's first production of the *Nutcracker* ballet took place here.

In September the San Francisco Opera House's opening night brings out the city's glitterati dressed to kill. The next day's *Chronicle* devotes pages to a description of who was wearing what. The opera season is followed by the ballet season. The San Francisco Ballet Company, founded in 1933, is actually America's oldest resident classical ballet company.

The 1997–98 opera season opened to a completely renovated Opera House with improved acoustics, re-gilded ceilings, reupholstered seats, polished chandeliers, seismic upgrading, better wheelchair accessibility, and, last but not least, more restrooms.

Continuing south on Van Ness, you come to the rounded glass and concrete Louise M. Davies Symphony Hall. Make sure to notice the Henry Moore sculpture *Large Four Piece Reclining Figure* in front. Constructed in 1980 and renovated in 1991, the ultramodern building contrasts with the more traditional style of the rest of Civic Center (except for the also-round State building).

Inside, the glass walls, huge open staircase, wide corridors, and the deck, where patrons can view the city sparkling at night, create a feeling of openness and space not usually associated with symphony halls. The acoustics were improved during the renovation and today are considered excellent. The Hall, which seats 2,743, is home to the San Francisco Symphony, whose season runs from October to May.

The Hall is also home to the Ruffatti Organ, which, with its 9,235 pipes, is the largest concert-hall organ in America.

GETTING BACK

Continue south to Market Street and turn left.

If you want to take a lunch break, stop at the fabulous and reasonably priced Ananda Fuara, a peaceful vegetarian restaurant at 1298 Market (corner of 9th). With its high ceilings and blue walls, this restaurant lives up to its name, which means in Bengali "Fountain of Supreme Bliss." However, don't expect this to be a five-minute lunch stop. People in bliss don't hurry.

After lunch, simply continue on Market to the cable car turnaround.

South Park & the Lefty O'Doul Bridge WALK 32

The South Park area has survived a number of historic convulsions. The actual park itself was developed in 1856 by George Gordon, a Gold Rush magnate, who planned to build fancy townhouses around the tiny grassy oval. At the time, South Park was a fashionable area, a next-door neighbor to exclusive Rincon Hill with its grand Victorian homes. Unfortunately for Gordon, the South Park neighborhood soon began its slide downward, and Gordon's plan was never realized. During the Longshoremen's strike of 1934, a virtual war was fought here, strikers and police doing actual battle in South Park itself.

Afterward, the area became home to many immigrant families who, along with drug dealers and winos, lived amid the growing number of warehouses and factories. In the 1980s the South Park was awakened from its general malaise by the gentrification overtaking San Francisco. Restaurants and cafés, boutiques and galleries began pushing out the "undesirables" and also many lower-income families who could no longer afford the rising rents.

The latest incarnation of the South Park area is as "multimedia gulch," home to numerous high tech firms—software designers, Web site creators, and CD ROM producers— who don't like Silicon Valley or who can't afford it.

Ordinarily, as you walk along, you can't detect the presence of these companies other than by the number of new restaurants and cafés. However, on December 14, 1995, almost 500 workers in this new "digitropolis" flooded into South Park to protest the proposed Communications Decency Act, which would have restricted freedom of expression over the Internet. (In 1997, the Act was declared unconstitutional by the U.S. Supreme Court.)

A wonderful side trip is to the Capp Street Project on the east end of the park at Second and Federal. This gallery shows installation art, which is art that's created for a specific site. In other words, when you enter the gallery, you enter into and become part of the art work. It's a fascinating place and worth many visits. And it's free!

WALKING TIME

If you go only to South Park, circle around it, and return to Hallidie Plaza, allow an hour and 10 minutes. If you want to explore the Capp Street Project, add the time you plan to spend inside this gallery. If you continue on to the Lefty O'Doul Bridge and walk across that, allow another 25 minutes, for a total walking time of an hour and 35 minutes. This does not include any time you spend browsing in the many outlet stores.

GETTING THERE

From the cable car turnaround at Market and Powell, cross Market and walk northeast on Market to Third. Turn right and go south on Third. You will pass through several, very different, districts. Past Mission is the heart of the city's new arts center, with Yerba Buena Gardens on your right and the San Francisco Museum of Modern Art on your left.

Across Howard, you will see the gigantic Moscone Convention Center—the size of six football fields. (Notice the ultra-modern street lights on Howard between Yerba Buena Gardens and the Convention Center.) Although the Center was expanded in 1991, it is still growing, with a huge children's center planned on the roof. Plans for the center include 130,000 square feet of outdoor play space, an ice-skating rink and bowling center, a child-care center, and a carousel rescued from Playland-at-the-Beach.

On the other side of Third, across from Moscone, notice the sculpture *Man with Flame* by Stephen de Staebler, a Saint Louis born artist who has sculpted in the Bay Area for many years, and also taught at San Francisco State University and the San Francisco Art Institute.

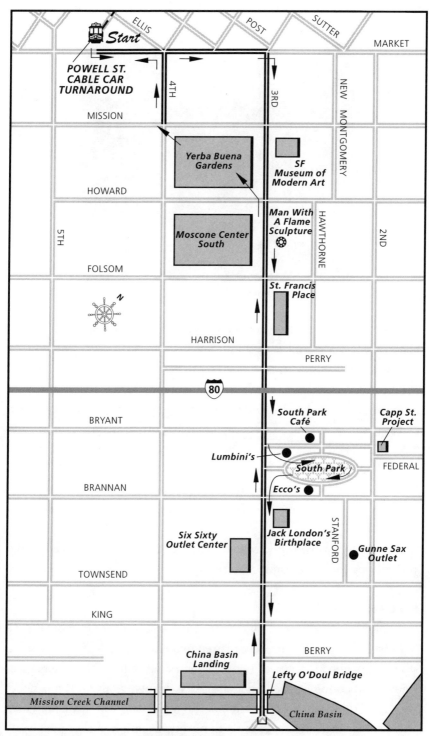

South Park and the Lefty O'Doul Bridge

The freeway sawed off at Perry Street

Across Folsom, on the east side of Third, you will come to fancy St. Francis Place, a complex of shops and luxury apartments, where many business travelers stay instead of going to hotels.

Across Harrison, the neighborhood became suddenly poorer and more rundown, the overhead freeway setting the gray tone. There are some clubs in this area, but not trendy ones. Reportedly, some multimedia-gulch workers do hang out at The Hotel Utah (500 Fourth Street) and at the Eagle (527 Bryant) but I haven't been in either place. On Perry Street, you can actually see where part of the freeway was chopped off after the Loma Prieta quake. "The edge of progress," as my brother would say.

Across Bryant, you will come to South Park Avenue. Glance left and you will see the actual park.

SOUTH PARK

It's a grassy oval so skinny that it's easy to miss entirely. Except for a few pieces of children's modern play equipment, the park looks like it has stood untouched for over a century, which essentially it has. There's definitely no parking garage under this place. Hanging out on the benches are a mixture of gentrification-surviving locals, multimedia-gulch techies, bike messengers, construction workers, and homeless people.

Walk around the park on the narrow sidewalk to glance into the shops and cafés. Lumbini's (156 South Park) is a garden and design shop containing an amazing collection of "stuff." As you continue around the park, you will come to Maison d'Etre (92 Jack London Alley) and Secret Gardens (64 South Park) which contain even more category-defying stuff. When I last looked into Maison d'Etre a gigantic, rusty suit of armor graced the window. Secret Gardens offered a fascinating tangle of fountains, benches, and plants.

The affluent can be relieved of their money at the South Park Café (108 South Park), which has the feel of a genuine Paris café, and the Ristorante Ecco (101 South Park), a chic Northern Italian restaurant where you will see people dressed in real business clothes—suits and ties for the men, nylons and high-heeled shoes for the women.

The houses around the Park look old. And largely unseen in these vintage Victorian dwellings and lofts surrounding you are the literally hundreds of multimedia companies that now call South Park "home."

THE CAPP STREET PROJECT

The Capp Street Project (525 Second), featuring site-related installation art, is open Tuesdays through Saturdays from noon to 6 P.M. Call before you go, because sometimes installations are being assembled or disassembled, and the gallery is closed when it's supposed to be open.

Enter the gallery around the corner on Federal Street and be prepared for an experience, as you will actually enter into the work of art. In a recent visit, I entered Ilya Kabakov's *The Hospital: Five Confessions*, which creates a journey through a Soviet asylum with its rough muslin curtains, sparse rooms, and bare overhead bulbs. Wandering the narrow corridors, I could hear the voices of patients mumbling fantastical stories to kindly doctors. Each installation is such a totally different experience that you will want to return here often.

THE LEFTY O'DOUL BRIDGE

After you leave South Park, you can return to the cable car turnaround and consider that you have had a respectable walk. Or you can take the next leg and continue to the Lefty O'Doul bascule bridge.

If you want to go on, continue south on Third and cross Brannan. The Wells Fargo Building on the southeast corner was the birthplace of Jack London on January 12, 1876. Of course, it wasn't a bank then; it was 615 Third, a dwelling destroyed in 1906 by the great fire.

As you continue on Third, you enter "discount heaven," San Francisco's clothing outlet neighborhood. Many of the outlets are clustered in 660 Third Street, an old brick building that was once an auction house. This building is also the home of HotWired.

For me, the best outlet store in the area is definitely the Gunne Sax outlet at 35 Stanford (between Second & Third and Brannan & Townsend). As a young mother, I clocked many hours here while my little daughters pulled bridal gowns and pinafores off the racks. In April and May the store is positively avalanched by soon-to-be brides and bridesmaids shopping for their wedding finery.

Continue south on Third and cross King and then Berry streets. Right before the bridge, you will see China Basin Landing (185 Berry) on your right. The back of this building opens onto the water and you can walk along here, breath some nautical air, and watch the occasional duck swim by.

You are now at the bridge.

The heavy weights of the Lefty O'Doul Bridge

The word *bascule* is the French word for seesaw, and, in fact, a bascule bridge is a drawbridge that work exactly like a seesaw. When the bridge must be raised to let a vessel pass underneath, huge weights descend on one end, raising the other end up. It's a little scary to stand under the huge weights, but so far, so good.

The bridge is named after Lefty O'Doul (1897–1969), a beloved San Francisco baseball legend and two-time National League batting champion, who played with and later managed the San Francisco Seals. The name of the bridge is quite fitting, since the new baseball stadium will be only a stone's throw (or a quick swim) away.

The original Third Street bascule bridge was built in 1904 by the Atchison, Topeka, and Santa Fe Railway Company and given to the city for free. The current bridge was built by Barrett & Hilp and opened May 12, 1933.

Walk across the bridge, cross carefully, and then walk back on the other side, so you can see both Mission Creek Channel to the west and China Basin to the east.

GETTING BACK

Go back the way you came, with this exception: when you get to Howard and Third, climb up the steps into Yerba Buena Gardens, and cross the Gardens diagonally to exit at Mission and Fourth. This will give you a moment of open space and air after the citified South of Market atmosphere. On Fourth, continue north to Market. Then turn left to return to the cable car turnaround.

St. Mary's Cathedral & Japantown

Small numbers of Japanese began arriving in San Francisco toward the end of the 19th century, settling in Chinatown and the south of Market area. After the '06 quake and fire, they moved into the old Victorians of the Western Addition, opening shops and restaurants.

Japantown was emptied in 1942 when its citizens were ordered into internment camps for the duration of World War II. After the war, their former homes occupied by others, many Japanese Americans moved to the suburbs. Others returned, forming the nucleus of today's *Nihonmachi*, or "Japantown."

This excursion actually comprises two walks: the first is along Geary to St. Mary's Cathedral; the second explores Japantown. You will see churches and temples of every faith and description. And you will see Victorians, Victorians, and more Victorians. In the Sixties—the bad old days of unenlightened urban renewal—22 blocks of Victorians were destroyed to create Japan Center, yet enough remain to provide an absorbing look at this ever-fascinating and fantastical architecture.

WALKING TIME

If you go only to St. Mary's Cathedral and back, allow a little under an hour. If you go on to Japantown, allow *at least* two hours.

GETTING THERE

The walk to St. Mary's Cathedral is lively and brisk, filled with the-aters, shops, tourists, restaurants, hotels, and galleries. Cathedral Hill gently rises to the west, with the majestic Roman Catholic Cathedral at its crest.

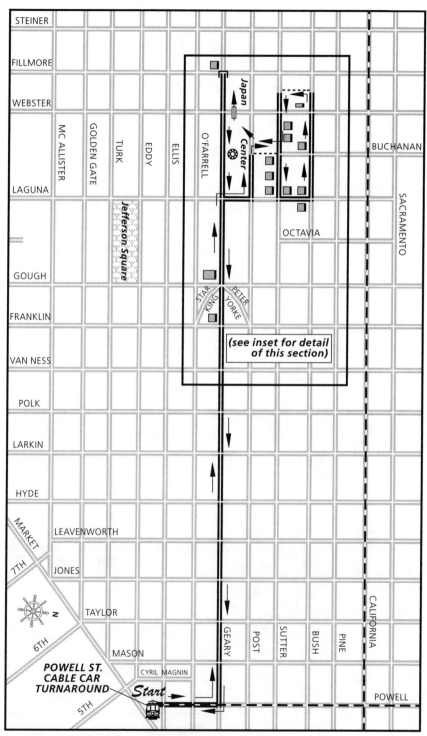

St. Mary's Cathedral and Japantown

From the cable car turnaround at Powell and Market, follow the cable car north along the tourist-drenched streets to Geary. You will see Union Square ahead on your right. Turn left.

Walking along Geary, you are in the heart of the theater and hotel district, with the historic Westin St. Francis hotel on your right. The entire block between Powell and Mason is flooded with art galleries. Across Mason are the Geary and Curran theaters, with huge David's Delicatessen awaiting the hungry theater-going crowd.

Across Taylor, head up hill, threading through the busy hotels and restaurants that service the tourist trade. You will pass Harold's International News Stand (524 Geary), a wonderful store where you can buy newspapers from practically anywhere in the world.

Across Jones, the neighborhood is less fancy, with grocery stores, bars, beauty parlors, thrift shops, and modest apartment buildings sprinkled in with the hotels. To your south is the Tenderloin, one of San Francisco's poorest neighborhoods and also its "sin city," complete with massage

BUSH

FILLMORE

11

10

14

13

BUCHANAN

9

8

SUTTER

OCTAVIA

N

FRANKLIN

12

WEBSTER

3 4 5 6

POST

Japan   Center

Peace
Pagoda

GEARY

PETER
YORKE
to the
CABLE CAR

1. First Unitarian Church
2. St. Mary's Cathedral
3. Nihonmachi Mall
4. JACL Headquarters

2

O'FARRELL

STAR
KING

1

15

5. Nichi Bey Kai Cultural Center
6. Sota Zen Mission Sokoji
7. Christ United Presbyterian Church
8. Old Bush St. Synagogue

ELLIS

GOUGH

9. KonKo Kye Church
10. Kimon Gakuen
11. Vollmer House
12. Cottage Row

LAGUNA

EDDY

13. Japanese Cultural Center
14. YWCA
15. Fillmore Auditorium

Jefferson Square

St. Mary's Cathedral and Japantown (inset)

The First Unitarian Church on Franklin and Geary

parlors, porno movies, and "adult" bookstores. Some of the Tenderloin atmosphere creeps over to Geary here, with an occasional massage parlor amidst the cafés.

You will pass the magnificent Alcazar Theater (650 Geary) built by the Shriners in 1917 as an Islamic Temple of the Shrine. It was converted to theater use in the late Fifties, and was remodeled by artistic director Steve Dobbins in 1990. The theater is a California Registered landmark.

Across Van Ness is Tommy's Joynt—a popular hofbrau and bar. With its wild decor, cheap food, and flowing beer, Tommy's Joynt has enjoyed immense popularity for all of its almost 50 years. Serving lots of buffalo meat, however, it's not the place for a vegetarian like me.

You're now officially climbing Cathedral Hill. At Franklin and Geary, you will come to the beautiful old stone First Unitarian Church (1187 Franklin). Built in 1888 and remodeled in 1968, this church has been active in the San Francisco community since before Gold Rush days. Its famous minister Thomas Starr King is buried at the corner of O'Farrell and Franklin in a white marble sarcophagus.

Continue to St. Mary's Cathedral (1111 Gough at Geary) at the crest of the hill.

ST. MARY'S CATHEDRAL

This towering monolith is the granddaughter of Old St. Mary's Cathedral, the simple church at California and Grant (see "Walk 10"). As the area around the original St. Mary's declined, merging into the infamous Barbary Coast, the church was moved to safer ground. In 1891 a new Cathedral was dedicated at Van Ness, but, this burned to the ground in 1962, so yet a third Cathedral, the present St. Mary's, was completed in 1971.

The gleaming white structure, finished in Italian travertine marble, rises 190 feet in the shape of a Greek cross. If services are not in progress, enter the Cathedral for an inspiring experience. Stand under the cupola, which is composed of four huge hyperbolic paraboloids. The thin stained glass windows above you form an overhead cross.

St. Mary's Cathedral at Gough and Geary

Look also at the poured concrete organ pedestal and, above the altar, the Richard Lippold sculpture composed of a shower of aluminum rods that rain light down upon the altar.

After you leave the Cathedral, walk around to look at the views of San Francisco to the south and west. Then you can return along Geary back to the cable car turnaround, or, if you're ready for more, go on to Japantown.

JAPANTOWN

Continue on Geary to Laguna. As you walk, you will see the Peace Pagoda come into view on the north side of Geary. At Laguna, cross Geary and walk one block to Post. Turn left. Enjoy the little shops along this block of Post. The Uoki Grocery store (1656 Post) has been run by the Sakai family for over a century.

At Post and Buchanan, you will see the Peace Pagoda on your left and Nihonmachi Mall (Buchanan Mall) on your right. You are in the center of Japantown.

The Nihonmachi Mall on Buchanan between Post and Sutter contains a series of circular benches designed by Ruth Asawa. Once there were fountains here too, but these are gone with only their rusty drains remaining. Today, pigeons, blackbirds, and running children fill the space inside of the benches in place of the water. Wonderful shops line the mall. My favorite is the Soko Hardware Company (1698 Post), which contains amidst the toilet seats, teapots, and paper lamps, a fascinating collection of Japanese saws.

At Sutter turn right. and walk past some gorgeous Victorian homes. At 1765 Sutter is the Japanese American Citizens League (JACL) headquarters. The JACL is a civil-rights organization working to ensure rights for Japanese Americans. During World War II, the organization lobbied for the formation of the volunteer Japanese American combat units that fought valiantly during the war. After the war, the JACL worked to combat prejudice against Japanese Americans.

Practically next door at 1759 is the Nichi Bey Kai Cultural Center with its lovely front garden. And on the corner of Sutter and Laguna, the Sota Zen Mission Sokoji (1691 Laguna), where students of Zen come to meditate. On the opposite corner is another religious institution, the Christ United Presbyterian Church (1700 Sutter).

Turn left on Laguna and walk north one block to the venerable, but crumbling, Bush Street Synagogue (1881 Bush). This landmark 1895 redwood building survived the '06 earthquake and fire. Originally, the building housed Congregation Ohabai Shalome, a Jewish group that broke from Congregation Emanu-El in 1863. In 1934 Ohabai Shalome disbanded, and since then, the synagogue has been used as a Zen center, a Christian church, and a club for playing the Japanese game of Go. The future use of the historic ex-synagogue is undecided, but a housing center for seniors is high on the list.

Across Laguna is the Konko Kye Church of San Francisco (1909 Bush), built in 1973. "Konko" means "teaching of the golden light." Founded in 1859 by a poor farmer named Ikigami Konko-Daijun, the religion teaches the idea of *Tenchi Kane no Kami*, the parent of the universe, existing in all things. Walk inside to feel the quiet simplicity.

Now look north down the 1800 block of Laguna to see magnificent Victorians, each more elaborate than the next. The ones on the west side are Stick-Eastlake style, so called because of the "sticks" that outline the windows and doors.

Turn left (west) on Bush, enjoying more gorgeous Victorians. At 2031 Bush is Kimon Gakuen, today the site of a Japanese pre-school. The gate on the left is where Japanese Americans assembled to leave for internment camp during World War II.

Continue on Bush to Webster. Then peer down Webster at the Vollmer House (1735-37 Webster). Built in 1885, this Stick-Eastlake Victorian is as ornate as it can get! The home was originally located on Turk near Franklin, but when that neighborhood was torn down in the seventies to build Opera Plaza, the Vollmer House was carted away and shoehorned into its present location.

Continue on Bush across Webster. Then, in the middle of the block, turn left into Cottage Row, another of San Francisco's mystical alleys that make you feel that you are the first to discover them. The alley is lined with simple Italianate row houses that date from the 1880s. Walk through the narrow red-bricked alley, past the tiny park on the right, and down the steps to Sutter.

Turn left (east) on Sutter and cross Webster again. On the south side of the street are more lovely Victorians. On the north side, the Japanese Cultural & Community Center of Northern California (1840 Sutter) offers cultural, educational, and social programs to the Japanese American community in this two-story building. Many community and non-profit organizations find a home here.

Right next door at 1830 Sutter is the Western Addition YWCA designed by Julia Morgan and built in 1912. This "Y" has traditionally served the Japanese community and is popularly know as the "Japanese Y." At the time of my writing, this building is the center of an enormous controversy between the owners, who want to sell the building to developers, and the Japanese American community, which contributed some of the initial construction money, and wants to keep the building for community use.

Continue on Sutter to Buchanan. Then turn right, walk through Buchanan Mall again, and cross Post to the Peace Pagoda. Designed by Professor Yoshiro Taniguchi, the Pagoda was donated to San Francisco by sister city Osaka. It has five tiers, which rise 100 feet above what was a reflecting pool, but which today is a garden.

From the Pagoda you can enter Japan Center, a three-building complex of restaurants and shops, which are connected by stairways and a bridge. The Center extends from Laguna to Fillmore and from Geary to Post. Two of my favorite shops are the Kinokunia Bookstore, which has a huge collection of Japanese and English books about Japan, and Townhouse Living, which offers beautiful paper lamps and intricate fountains. Both are in the Kinokunia Building. The adventurous might want to try the Kabuki Hot Springs (1750 Geary), a traditional Japanese bathhouse offering both private and communal baths.

The Center also contains the Kabuki Theater, where sometimes I like to sneak away from work early, meet my husband, and take in a movie.

Exit Japan Center at Geary and Fillmore. Cross both Geary and Fillmore to get a look at the historic Fillmore Auditorium (1807 Geary), where the late Bill Graham held rock concerts, and where once in the Sixties I....well, never mind.

214 ■ LUNCHTIME WALKS IN DOWNTOWN SAN FRANCISCO

GETTING BACK

To get back, just walk east on Geary all the way back to Powell, and then head south three blocks to the cable car turn around.

Or jump on the 38 Geary bus and get to Powell Street fast.

Index